FROM SIXPENCES
TO DOLLARS

FROM SIXPENCES TO DOLLARS

JANET LEE

APEX PUBLISHING LTD

First published in 2009 by
Apex Publishing Ltd
PO Box 7086, Clacton on Sea, Essex, CO15 5WN

www.apexpublishing.co.uk

British Library Cataloguing-in-Publication Data
A catalogue record for this book
is available from the British Library

ISBN 1-906358-41-9 978-1-906358-41-9

Typeset in 11.5pt Baskerville Win95BT

Production Manager: Chris Cowlin

Cover Design: Siobhan Smith
Cover Photo: Jamie Cooper, Chase Post

Printed by the MPG Books Group in the UK

Dedication by Janet Lee

Dedicated to my dad (non gambler) Arthur Raymond Hicks for his kindness and silly humour. I miss him terribly.

Dedication by Jonny Texas

Dedicated to all the mothers, fathers, wives and children of gamblers.

Contents

Foreword by Dave 'Devilfish' Ulliott

My first dealing with Jonny Hewston was in the Victoria Casino, Edgeware Road, London when I bought a ten per cent piece of him at a main event.

Jonny won it and I collected £3,000.

After that we became great friends.

This led me to ask him to play poker in the England team when I was given the job as Captain. It was my task to pick the team and it was a tough job to do. For every one you pick there are 20 others you can't. It's not a job you get thanked for.

I picked Jonny because of his tremendous record in the one table format.

He duly won the England game. He also won the support of me and all of his family - and I know he was very proud. This was also a great result for me. By the way, I'd like to say in poker about 15% of players win, but in holdem luck and skill are around 50/50. In other games, i.e. stud, the skill level is higher. In casinos and betting shops the odds of winning are much worse!

This was also a great result for me.

Jon strikes me as a loveable rogue, a type of guy not unlike Del Boy of TV's Only Fools and Horses.

Like Del, Jon's heart is in the right place.

I wish him success with the book - which is a damn good read.

Introduction by Janet Lee

The first time I heard of Jonny was when I met a young man in Cannock who was really excited because this poker player had turned up at a local pub event.

Having Jonny there it seemed, really made the night.

Working as a local newspaper reporter I interviewed Jonny about his appearance at the poker night.

And after the interview he told me people often said he should write a book, because of the extraordinary life he has led.

So here we are.

Jonny and I spent a year of interview sessions, and what you have here is his story in his words.

There have been times when I have looked incredulously at him and said: "You did WHAT?" He has been a very bad boy at times.

He is a contradictory character, as you will see. He can be exasperating and endearing in equal measures.

Trying to get his undivided attention is impossible. He can be talking on the phone or gambling on three different games at the same time as being interviewed.

Jonny's saving grace is his humour and love of his family.

I started this journey knowing nothing whatsoever about poker.

But whether you're a poker player or not I hope you enjoy his extraordinary story.

Introduction by Jonny Texas

I have seen so much heartache that I don't want people to get the impression that being a professional poker player appearing on TV is something anyone can do.

They can't.

I know a guy, who has a family, who packed in his £20,000 a year job to be a poker player. He is on his arse now.

There are kids of 20 dropping out of college to play poker and ending up with nothing.

This is the reason I am writing this book.

For every 20,000 players there will be only about 30 winners.

You can have a guy who is very good and very experienced – but it's still down to luck.

The reason one guy has got the edge is because every time he bets he has a good hand.

It would be the same in a football match. If the footballers were all in disguise you might think you could take them on.

But if it were Beckham in disguise – you'd have no chance.

We have got to start taking gambling seriously.

When you see those great big casinos in Las Vegas, just remember they have been built with money from the losers, not the winners.

Every betting shop and bingo hall is built on losers. There's no winners' money there.

There have been more lows than highs in my life - you'll see that. And no matter what people might think, the only way I make money is through the poker site. You can't make money by gambling. Take my word for it.

Chapter 1
The Seeds are sown

I'm sitting in a room full of people playing cards and the cash is flowing.

I watch fascinated as their mood changes when they win or lose. I see elation, laughter, fun, disappointment, camaraderie. It's a real atmosphere when this bunch of people come together - a time of excitement and fascination.

I'm five years old.

Friends and family have got together. And they may only be playing for pennies, but it may as well be thousands.

Anyway I was already an old hand at gambling. For the past year I'd been visiting the betting shop, another place of wonder.

My childminder, an Asian woman, was a regular there.

As a four-year-old I absolutely loved everything about the place: the writing on the board (though I didn't know what 'odds' meant), and people shouting and coming out with little tickets. I can still remember the smoky atmosphere.

So you see, even from a young age, the seeds were sewn.

I was born Jon Hewston in a little flat at 28 Underhill Road, Alum Rock, Birmingham on 17th August 1962. Dad owned the flat. Though I was too young to realise, life was strange right from the start.

My mum Phyllis and dad Harry weren't married. And in those days that was strictly taboo. To make matters worse, mum had been married before and had a daughter, my elder sister Stephanie, from that marriage.

Even worse: dad was still married to someone else - and already had four children.

Mum worked in dad's hairdresser's shop and I was the result of an affair.

Then they had another child together, my other sister Samantha, who was born a year after me.

Me, mum and my older sister all lived in that little flat where I was born. Then when I was three years old, dad bought us a semi, next to a shop at 66 Birmingham Road, Water Orton, Birmingham.

He didn't marry mum - and still kept his other family going. As kids, we had no idea about dad's other family.

I only saw my dad once or twice a week, but was too young to realise why. Mum said he was at night school. When I did see him he was gambling with his friends at our house.

With my child's logic (and we're talking about age three, four or five here) I figured if I gambled I would see more of my dad!

I think the first time I actually won pennies was sitting on his lap playing three card brag. As a little kid ending up with a handful of pennies I was just so excited.

Dad was a gambler, so I guess gambling was already in my blood.

Despite our strange lifestyle, as an adult I look back with

some admiration. Dad actually did a good job looking after two 'ordinary' working class families and I have a lot of respect for him.

Little did I know then, that this had a lot to do with the experiences he had with his own father. But more of that later.

It may sound odd now, but this was normal life for me. Even at that young age I could see the effect that money had on people. It intrigued me that money could have control on people's mood swings. People were happy when they won; sad when they lost. Money can be the making of people, but can also be the root of all evil and bring about their downfall. People can be bought. I learnt that at about the age of five.

At that age there were other influences. My Uncle Ronnie (by dad's other marriage) used to turn up at our working class house in a Rolls Royce. He always wore the most expensive new watches - and as a kid I was very impressed. I didn't know then how he got these possessions.

Flash cars, beautiful watches: I thought that was what life was all about.

And there was 'Doc', a friend of dad's. At least he said he was a doc' when I cut my finger at the age of six. His name was Alec Logan, and he was to feature largely in my life.

But even in adulthood I called him Doc until the day he died.

I couldn't wait to grow up. I realised there were things out there. But in the meantime I was happy to be excited about having an orange in my Christmas stocking, having our first colour TV, man landing on the moon and England winning the world cup.

I had a difficult start at school, and it took a while before anyone realised I couldn't see the blackboard.

I had to have glasses, and as I was a clumsy child that wasn't good because I was constantly breaking them.

When I broke yet another pair, my dad finally lost his temper and chose the hot water bottle to wallop me with. Unfortunately it broke and the scalding water burnt me so badly I ended up in hospital.

But some good did come out of it. All my classmates wrote to me, and at such a young age that made me feel really important.

Even as a child in woodwork class I had a one track mind. I remember a cube of wood falling on the floor. To me it was obvious what to do with it.

I turned it into a hand made dice!

As a six year old I had to content myself with gambling for sweets. Kevin Dobson used to bring sweets to school every day. And every day I'd win them off him!

But even at that age my mum thought there was something 'special' about me.

She tells the story about the time she lost her favourite earring in our garden. I remember the occasion, because I couldn't bear to see her upset. Then I hit on an idea. Bear in mind I was still only six!

I remembered looking out of the school window one day and seeing a man with a metal detector. I didn't know what it was until I asked the teacher.

She told me the man was 'looking for lost treasure'. I

went up to the man and told him about my mum being upset. He actually turned up at our house in his Rolls Royce with his metal detector to look for mum's earring!

Unfortunately, our house was built on a plot where all the rubble was buried, so his detector was beeping constantly!

He didn't find the earring. But the thought was there ...

I was really close to my mum, perhaps because I didn't have a full time dad there. Even as a kid I would save half my bar of chocolate for her and had to be dragged to school screaming.

I remember once when I was about six mum fell over in the street and cut her knee. A man laughed at her when she fell and I was so incensed that I just wanted to kill him. Mum was beautiful - and she tells me to let you know she still is!

But when I was little she developed septicaemia and had to go to hospital. Her sister, my Aunty Jackie looked after me - another female family member I was close to. Sadly Aunty Jackie was with a man who used to beat her. I saw a lot of that.

I was also close to my grandmother, my mum's mum.

I can still remember my great great grandfather, mum's grandad, who used to visit. He wore an 'old man's' hat under which he'd hide extra strong mints for me. He was always setting me some challenge.

I lived in an airy fairy world as a child. I don't know if everyone else is the same, but I could conjure up a whole different world in my mind. I could be playing with my cars, but be in a completely different city, living life as a famous driver!

At eight years old I even had a bet with one of the other kids on the results of a school football match. Unfortunately, I was playing in one of the teams - and I scored an own goal on purpose to win the bet ...

I remember we lost 15:14. Match fixing at such a tender age.

But I did grow up quickly.

I was smoking at the age of eight or nine - and cigarettes became the next currency, especially as you could buy them one at a time for 2p. It was easy. You could always get your hands on four or five pennies.

My sister Samantha was oblivious to all this. She had her own circle of friends. Perhaps that was just as well then. Unlike me, she went on to get 'A' levels and a degree.

There are some nice memories.

When I was eight at Water Orton First School I was part of a 48-hour snakes and ladders marathon, which actually made it into the Guinness Book of Records!

I still drive back to Water Orton sometimes and park outside the junior school for a quiet reminisce. There were a lot of unanswered questions in my childhood.

At nine years old I remember finding £15. I could have easily kept it, but I handed it into a police station. It turned out to be a guy's savings, and when he claimed the money he came round to our house and gave me 50p. You see money wasn't always important to me then.

I was quite lonely as a child.

Like most kids I had a nickname. Mine was Hewston Station! Later on kids started calling me Texas.

But all was well when I watched my family happy playing cards.

It's only now when I analyse things that I realise how many influences were there.

Dad was very strict with us, very hard. He never played games with us. But even today he would lay his life down for me and I love him to bits. He has got me out of many scrapes.

It was only as I got a bit older that I realised that our family wasn't quite normal.

The word 'bastard' was commonplace then - and it was used in the true sense of the word. I started to find it embarrassing that my parents weren't married. I couldn't possibly tell other people, and I felt dirty (they actually didn't marry until I was 15 years old).

At nine years old I discovered something absolutely wonderful - the horse racing game Totopoly!

There were little metal horses and you could bet on the winner. They were such real horses to someone like me.

And there was monopoly with 'real' money!

Oh how the world seemed to open up to me.

Looking back, my life was strange. But little did I know then, that it would become much stranger.

Chapter 2
My Dad

So imagine this.

One Sunday dad says he going to take us for a drive. I was about ten or 11 at the time.

We ended up visiting Elmdon Airfield in Birmingham and I was just beside myself with excitement to see all those planes.

We actually got close up to a Piper Cherokee and all I could think about was how fantastic it would be if I could just sit in a seat in that plane.

Imagine how thrilled I was when my sister Samantha and I were able to sit in the back of this plane, with mum in the front.

Then dad jumped into the pilot's seat, pulled the seat forward, put headphones on him and mum, shut the door - and we flew off!

All I could think of was 'what is he doing the silly old sod? He can't take this up in the air'.

But dad was a pilot and I never knew! Suddenly, to me, dad had become a fighter pilot, a hero. I was just so proud.

He flew us over the Welsh mountains - to the sounds of Johnny Mathis singing Come Fly With Me on the radio!

So that was where he was every night when I thought he was at night school. He was learning to fly!

After that it became quite a regular thing.

It turned out dad was part of a syndicate of three men who owned the plane. Sadly one of them crashed it in Staffordshire, so that was the end of that.

Dad asks me to this day why I don't learn to fly.

All in all dad had some strange and unpredictable traits.

One day he came home on a motorbike, which I thought was hypocritical since he wouldn't allow me to have a pushbike. He didn't like the idea of kids riding bikes on the road. He thought that was too dangerous.

My mate had a pushbike. I can remember it now. It was immaculate, purple in colour with gears, which you could change.

I was about nine or ten at the time, and one day I pleaded with my mate: "Please can I just SIT on it?"

He agreed, but the instant I sat on the saddle I spotted my dad driving towards us in his van. He came up to me, his face like thunder.

All my mate saw was this man come up to me, throw me off the bike, hurl the bike 300ft into the air across a hedge into a field, then drive off! He had no idea it was my dad, and just looked horrified. To this day I have never seen a bike thrown so far! After that my mate was scared to let me ever even sit on his bike.

When I had kids of my own I didn't want them to have a bike - but my wife just told me to stop being so silly!

Chapter 3
High School

I used to tell everyone I went to Coleshill Grammar School.

Well that was true in a way.

In those days you had to pass the 11 plus exam to get into grammar school. I failed it.

But the school was in the process of changing from a grammar to a 'high' school when I started there, so I chose to say I went to grammar school.

I don't think I was particularly naughty or violent at school, but I managed to get into trouble in other ways.

As I got older I thought 'I don't need education. I know where I'm going'. I just knew I was going to be wealthy, but didn't know how. That was the intriguing part.

I was bursting with ideas how to make money - and I realised how many suckers there were out there.

Looking back, I was developing into a con man. Even if the other kids wouldn't gamble with me I would get money out of them in other ways. That's not something I'm proud of now. But gambling was like a drug.

I was gambling at every opportunity in various ways. I became a fight promoter at school, trading cigarettes or sweets as bets. Whatever was going on, I was at the middle of it.

I organised arm wrestling competitions, boxing matches, fishing contests in the school pool - all with the aim of placing bets of course.

Once I organised a high jump competition between me and another kid. I bet him two quid I could beat him. Little did he know, me and my mate had tied an almost invisible fishing line to the bar, and every time he thought he'd cleared it we yanked it off! He just could not understand why the bar kept coming off. We made it the 'best of three'.

On one occasion I had a bet with a kid for £5 million. He never paid me - so he still owes me £5m!

It was all just a challenge, a gamble. But the word 'gamble' to me meant winning and succeeding, not losing. Even today I don't know any other way to interpret the word.

The teachers were well aware what I was up to. I was never caned and had reports, which said things like 'Jon is an interesting member of class', 'Jon can be disruptive', or 'Jon feels he knows more than the teachers'!

The last straw was when I locked myself in a cupboard in the school hall while an exam was going on, to see how long it would take teachers to find me - for a bet of course.

But I coughed, so I was discovered.

I was 'asked to leave' the school. OK, I was expelled.

I moved to a school, which was actually nearer my home.

The buzz around my new school was 'Texas is coming'.

Chapter 4
Oh Brother

It was around this time that I had a surprise introduction - to my dad's younger brother. I remember playing in the alleyway of our house when dad turned up and a man got out of the car.

Dad said: "I want you to meet somebody. It's my brother Colin."

I was absolutely in awe and simply said 'hello'.

We really hit it off, and I thought it was fantastic having this new uncle. Dad never explained why I hadn't met him before.

We went everywhere together, played football and he stayed overnight at our house.

One day dad drove us to a house in nearby Pype Hayes to meet a family. It was only later in my life I discovered this family had previously lived just down the road from us in Water Orton. But I didn't realise the significance at the time.

There was a woman at the house - I remember she was cleaning the curtains when I first met her.

Dad introduced her. "This is my mum Mavis," he said. Again there was no explanation as to why I hadn't met my 'grandmother' before. I actually used to ask her what my dad was like as a little boy.

Mavis was lovely to me. Over the next few years I was to stay at her house often with my newly found uncle. There were three girls living at the house: Heather, Angela and Linda - in their teens, but all older than me.

Gradually things fell into place and the penny dropped.

I would hear the girls and my 'uncle' call my dad 'dad'.

One day Colin just said to me: "He's my dad as well."

What a bombshell. My world was already strange.

Colin and the girls were my half brother and half sisters.

Mavis was dad's 'other woman'. This was the other family I had never met.

I was pleased I had a brother, because as a child I played with my sisters' Tiny Tears dolls and would be knitting with my mum - the ultimate, ultimate, mummy's boy.

My sister Samantha preferred to play with a hammer and nails.

But even though I liked Colin, I felt hurt and resentful.

I particularly felt for my mum because I was so close to her.

To this day, dad still hasn't properly explained the family set-up to me. The task fell to Colin.

I remember one day dad brought a baby back to our house for us to see. He said it was his sister's child.

I remember mum asking him: "You do love our kids as well?"

How sad when you look back.

Dad never let on that the baby was his grandchild - from his 'other family'.

Chapter 5
Little Tex at School

After being expelled I was accepted at Park Hall School - where all my dad's kids from the other family went, including my newly found brother.

He was known as 'Texas' at the school, so I naturally became 'Little Tex'.

When I was at school I didn't like being called Jonny, because that was Durex!

Incidentally, Colin turned out to be ten times worse than me as a gambler. More about him later ...

Things were no better for me at this school. I simply could not understand why people wanted to be educated. I found it strange, so I was very destructive.

I was only interested in sport and cookery, so didn't concentrate and fell behind academically.

My mum still has a report from my science teacher - 'Jon takes no interest whatsoever in the lesson - but his cheese scones are great'!

I was soon up to my old tricks: smoking, and gambling with dice games and football cards. And I always got caught at it.

When I was called into the headmaster's office I thought 'now I AM in a dilemma'.

I was expelled again.

All I could do was beg Coleshill High to take me back, which they did. I decided I really must settle - but I was fixing athletics and swimming matches (for money of course) and I was expelled again.

When I got home I remember saying: "I feel like just killing myself."

My dad was so furious he actually offered me a knife!

It wasn't until years later I realised why he was so angry.

My grandad had actually killed himsefl at an eraly age, in his early 30s. It was in the 1930s, when the recession was on in Great Britain. He found it hard to cope with his drink and gambling problems and took the easy way out by hanging himself. My father always said he was a coward for leaving a young wife and three young children. Obviously, if I had realised this I never would have said it; but this is a part of growing up. You regret things you say to people, it's part of the process of 'think before you speak'.

I remember later in life going to my gran's grave and seeing my grandad's stone there. It felt very earie to see 'Harry Hewston', the same name as my dad. All this gave me more of a solid respect for my dad, realising what kind of life he had - losing his father at wight years old, then later bringing up two families. It is only now I realise what a really hard life he had.

Throughout my problems at school mum never showed how hurt she must have been.

Chapter 6
Up to Tricks

We were on the move again - and I was mortified.

Dad moved us to the more upmarket Wylde Green where he ran a fruit and vegetable shop with his mate/business partner Alec Logan ('Doc' to me). We lived in the flat above.

For the first time, dad actually moved in with us as a family.

I did not want to leave my mates, so I thought we could at least have a farewell do.

I decided to organise a party at Water Orton 'town hall' - actually a community centre. Everyone was up for the party, which was going to be a huge event.

They all agreed to donate some money towards the hire of the hall etc and I collected the money from everyone. On the day of the party they all turned up - to find the hall doors locked. They all just stood outside.

I had taken all their money and gambled it away. There was no party. This was the worse thing that ever happened to me because it left such a bad taste.

They still talk about it in Water Orton. Even now they'll come up to me and say 'remember the party?'

Back in Wylde Green I had to make new friends, and I dreaded it because I thought everyone was stuck up.

But I always had fags, so that bought me new mates. I bought the fags with money I nicked from the fruit shop.

I went to Boldmere High and staggered through to the end of my school days getting up to the same tricks - and the teachers were fully aware of my 'gambling problem'.

There were a lot of fights (as in I'll beat you for a tenner).

I remember there was a Chinese kid. I was convinced I could beat him easily in a fight so took out a bet with him.

He turned out to be a Kung Fu expert!

Another time I got my arse whooped was when I had a fight with a lad at summer camp. I thought he was a geek: a spotty, swotty kid. But he was about 6ft 3in and 16 stone. His sheer weight when he jumped on me won the fight. I was so embarrassed.

I was always very accident-prone. Once I got a ball bearing ring stuck on my finger and spent hours in the hospital while it was greased off.

Then I cut my hand with a chisel, and while I was recovering at home, cut my other hand gardening.

One morning I had stomach ache, but my dad made me walk to school. There was a funeral taking place nearby. Dad thought I was being over dramatic when I told him I was so ill that could be me. Anyway, it turned out I had a rumbling appendix, so I had to be rushed to hospital.

It was while I was at Boldmere High, when I was 15, that mum and dad gave me a wedding invitation.

It was to their wedding.

It took place at Birmingham Register Office - and was a mixture of happiness and embarrassment.

School days ended in typical fashion.

I should have done my ‘o’ levels as they were then.

But I simply didn’t turn up.

Mum and dad had so many problems with me that around this time I lived in a bedsit in Erdington where one of my half sisters lived.

I stayed there for a few months because I could no longer live at home.

There seemed no certainty about anything at the time.

Sometimes I didn’t know where the next pound or meal was coming from.

Mum and dad had simply had enough. From the ages 13-15 I was very rebellious; at 14 I was a habitual gambler. I knew nothing else. I was fascinated by fruit machines or any challenges.

I believe it was actually an addiction - an addiction to a challenge, something I will talk about later. As a kid I was always seeking a thrill or a buzz.

But I wasn’t greedy. In fact I gave a lot of my money away.

Anyway one day after school I called to see mum and dad at their house - to find they had gone on holiday with my sister to America without telling me. Because of my behaviour I understood why.

Now when I look back there are a lot more things I understand.

Eventually I did move back in with mum and dad.

Chapter 7
The world of work

My first job was as a part time petrol pump attendant on Saturdays while I was still at school. It was at a garage in Chester Road, Erdington, Birmingham.

By this time we had gone up in the world and moved again - to a nice house in Antrobus Road, Sutton Coldfield.

Next I worked cleaning cars at a garage in Wylde Green. Well, I was supposed to be cleaning the cars, but I actually became quite skilled at selling them. I discovered I had quite a talent as a salesman.

One day the boss, Ron Morton called me into his office. My talent had not gone unnoticed and he offered me a full time job as a salesman when I left school. I took him up on his offer and was delighted to receive my first weekly wage of £17.25. I was actually getting cash of my own at last.

Because I was so young other salesman had to work the books. I would do the sales and they would get the cash for me. But the more cars I sold, the more they would benefit too.

Suddenly, we were beating other branches' figures and word was getting around. In the end they had no option but to start paying me more.

But, as was to become a pattern, I just couldn't get to work on time - and despite my high sales record I was sacked. I lasted four months.

Then I got a job at Tesco in Erdington when I was 17. I was led to believe this was as a trainee assistant manager. But in actual fact there were about ten of us, all doing the same job - in the warehouse. Suffice to say I met some really nasty characters there.

So far in my life I had tried to mix with all age groups. I particularly believed that I could learn from older folk. But it was during this job that I came to realise not all of them deserved to be respected and looked up to, just because they were older.

There were some real numbskulls. So I learnt at an early age that there were many people older than me who actually weren't that bright. In fact, they were stupid.

The manager of the store was sacked for stealing a bottle of whiskey. Another employee came to work in his old trainers and walked out with new ones - and got caught. It wasn't the nicking that I found appalling, just the stupidity that they got caught.

People pinch all the time off their employers. Everybody does it, wherever they work, even if they just pinch time from their employer.

I felt as if I had been duped into this job. And I remember thinking 'I've got to go and look for the smart people. They have got to be out there'.

Now I know that all the smart, rich people in the world have made mistakes in the early stages.

As usual I was borrowing money left right and centre for gambling. I owed money to lots of people, including employees at Tesco. I borrowed the money and somehow just could not get in front. But I didn't even feel bad about it. I felt people owed it to me for some reason. I owed about £120 - which was a lot of money in those days.

My parents were aware of it - and so was dad's mate/business partner Alec 'Doc' Logan.

Doc, who has always played a large part in my life, picked me up one day from Tesco in his red Jag. (Incidentally, I am now the proud owner of a red Jag - inspired by Doc).

But it was clear Doc was in no mood for chitchat. In fact he was in such a scary mood that I was petrified.

Instead of driving me home, he drove to the gates of Swinfen Hall - a young offenders' institute near Lichfield. He physically dragged me out of the car by the scruff of my neck, punched me in the face, ripped my shirt off and bellowed: "This is where I ended up at your age." I just wanted to get home. I thought he was going to kill me.

Doc realised the stress I was causing my mom and dad and was furious. This was his way of telling me the direction I was heading in.

He made me tell him everyone I owed money to and how much. Then he did a marvellous thing. He drove me round to them all and paid off all the debts - all £120 of it.

"I'm not doing this for you," he said. "I'm doing it for your dad."

That wiped the slate clean and took a lot of stress off me.

My next job was at a furniture store in Erdington High Street.

I particularly remember that time. All the news was of the murder of paperboy Carl Bridgewater.

I enjoyed working as a salesman there, but I had the worst timekeeping in the world, and after about three months I got the sack - again.

I also had an attitude: everyone was wrong and I was right. I knew more than them, so would not listen. Now of course I realise that people were just trying to help me. I think people actually liked me, that is why they bothered trying to help.

And of course I even owed money to people at the shop.

My next job, at the age of 19, was as a grill chef at the Royal Hotel, Sutton Coldfield.

To my delight my boss was a gambler - and there was a betting shop in Sutton Coldfield. So that was my wages down the pan. We were betting on horses, so I was usually about three weeks behind with my wages. I did have some good wins along the way though.

I wasn't gambling just for the sake of it. Gambling gave me an adrenaline rush, like a drug, like Prozac. It was never about the money - more to do with a chemical reaction in the brain.

There have now been all kinds of tests carried out to try and get to the bottom of why people gamble, and I'll talk about this later in the book.

Back to being a grill chef where my claim to fame was cooking a steak for Alfredo Berni - he of Berni Inns fame.

I might have only been throwing chips and beans on a plate, but I actually enjoyed that job. It was at the hotel that I met John McGonagle who was to become a great friend. He would often come into the bar and we would have long chats there. I will tell you more about him later.

But it was John who said to me in that bar: "One day you will be successful and on TV." Sadly, he is no longer with us, but I like to think he is over there watching me.

I would often meet John outside the hotel. On one occasion he told me about a guy in Sutton Coldfield who was facing a court appearance over a garage burglary and needed an alibi.

His name was 'Phil the Skin' - and he was prepared to pay £300. My gambling urge kicked in: anything to earn a deal.

I started looking for Phil the Skin and managed to track him down in Sutton Coldfield.

I told him I could give him a good alibi that would get him off. He paid me £300 in pound notes. It was so much money then.

As has often been the case with particular people I met in strange circumstances, little did I realise then that Phil would feature largely in my life later. If only I had known then that he was to become my brother-in-law 25 years later!

But I didn't know. So, having no intention of providing him with an alibi I went in hiding for weeks. I didn't care. I had an attitude - and people like Phil didn't scare me.

My job at the hotel came to a dramatic end when there was a fire in the hotel kitchen. I ran and grabbed a bucket, of what I thought was water, and threw it on the fire.

But the bucket contained about 50 knives and forks - which ricocheted back like arrows and nearly stabbed a woman in the eye!

That was the end of my stint as a grill chef.

Incidentally, I am proud to say that hotel is now owned by a friend of mine - and runs Jonny Texas poker nights every week!

Chapter 8
Living like a lord and a policeman

I had £300, a lot of money for a 19-year-old. What better to do with it than gamble it?

I went to Cromwell's Casino in Corporation Street, Birmingham, and played a two-card French game called Baccaro, where you have to choose whether to be banker or player.

I left the casino with £10,000! Enough to buy about five houses in Erdington at the time!

But I chose to spend it in a very different way.

I went to a posh local hotel, hired out a complete floor and lived like a lord for three days with the casino staff. We partied all night and I paid for champagne, drinks and food for everyone.

Dad heard about it and went to the hotel - naturally expecting to have to foot the £1,800 bill. But when he arrived he was told the bill had been settled. I had paid it.

Ironically I shouldn't have been in the club in the first place because I wasn't old enough.

The staff were all sacked and I was banned from the club.

Four days later I had lost the rest of the money at a

betting shop.

I didn't even care that I lost it. I didn't care that gambling was frowned on. It had given me a taste of what I wanted.

To this day I still look back at the time I lived like a lord for three days. But my luck was to be short-lived. My next escapade got me in trouble with the law.

I was working with a mate as a street salesman by now, selling jewellery out of suitcases for two wealthy Londoners who drove around in Rolls Royces.

But they were not paying us as they should.

One day I went with one of the Londoners to deposit some jewellery at a shop in Erdington for repairs. I noticed exactly what item of jewellery he had taken there.

Me and my mate reckoned we would get our own back. After all, we were owed money.

So we put on smart black suits and white shirts and went into the shop. We told the shopkeeper we were policemen, and had heard he may have jewellery there, which had been stolen. I was able to describe the jewellery exactly, and the shopkeeper confirmed he did have that piece there.

We told him the item belonged to someone and we wished to return it. He was delighted he was able to help us. We left the shop - and sold the jewellery to get our wages owed.

I was in trouble again - charged for impersonating a policeman.

When the case went to court my solicitor made much of my gambling 'problem', so the magistrate ordered me to attend Gamblers Anonymous.

I went to the meeting, which was held in Birmingham. I could hardly get my breath when I heard the others confess their 'problems'. One guy couldn't resist putting 2ps in fruit machines; another gambled on golf matches with his mate, another on the horses.

Big deal!

As far as I was concerned they didn't know what a gambling 'problem' was - until they met me.

We were supposed to be there to support each other. But as far as I was concerned, I was listening to a load of losers.

"You know what your problem is?" I said to them. "You need to go to a casino!"

I took them all to a local casino. One guy had managed to stay off gambling for two years until he met me.

Suffice to say - I was 'asked to leave' Gamblers Anonymous.

But I still thought I knew best, I knew more than they did.

That was just me.

Chapter 9
Snookered

My brushes with the law continued as I got into petty crime.

One of my most memorable crimes could be entered into a dumbest criminals programme to be shown on TV for all to laugh at.

I had gone to play snooker with some mates at a hall in Sutton Coldfield, but I had a long wait to play on the table. So to pass the time I started playing the fruit machine - and was really peed off that the machine had 'enticed me' into losing £60. I would have preferred to have used some of that money to play snooker.

Anyway, I waited for the owner to lock up then I went back, with the intention of getting 'my' £60 back.

I broke a window and got in through the fire exit door.

I managed to get my £60 out of the back of the machine - plus 'interest'.

Then I reasoned that because I missed out on my snooker game I'd catch up on it now. So I switched the lights on, made myself a coffee - and played snooker for five hours!

Inevitably I was caught.

The case went to court and I was fined £70 - plus had to pay back the money I had taken. I was done for breaking and entering - and 'criminal damage' to the machine.

The newspaper headlines read 'Burglar stops to Play Snooker!'

Needless to say, I was very embarrassed.

I thought at one point that I could give up being a burglar and earn money by playing snooker instead. At the time I needed money for gambling, so I funded it by petty crime such as receiving stolen goods.

I also managed to make a prat of myself at work.

By this time the only person who would employ me was my dad. He had opened several clothes shops called Bandwagon. His business partner was actually the legendary comedian Arthur Askey who provided financial backing. The shops were named after Arthur's popular radio show at the time.

I was working in the warehouse of dad's Newtown shop in Birmingham and had been there for about nine months.

Darts was the in thing at the time, so never one to miss a trick, I built a wall out of a stack of boxes and held organised darts matches behind it with the staff - for money of course.

During one of the matches, one of the guys said: "Just imagine if your dad saw us now."

"He wouldn't sack me. I'm his son," I said.

But just like that time he turned up out of the blue and caught me riding the bike, he was even then standing behind me.

"You're sacked," he said.

The strange thing was, I got home and dad was sitting

on the settee. It was just as if he was two separate people.

As if it was a perfectly normal thing to say he said: "Hello son. Had a good day at work?"

"No. I got the sack!" I told him.

I went through a period where I thought I just would not be able to get a job anywhere.

It really seemed to me at that time in my life that gambling had got a really big hold of me and that I could see no future for me.

Dad was a successful businessman and I could not even get hold of a job at his company.

It just seemed like the big win was going to come - but the big win never comes! It's a dream that you have as a gambler.

I think it was at that stage I realised this could be a rocky road.

Chapter 10
House of Celebs

We were definitely going up in the world.

Dad's business was going great and we were moving to increasingly bigger and better houses.

By the time I was 20 I was rubbing shoulders with the rich, the famous and the infamous.

Barbara Windsor, of Carry On fame, lodged with mum and dad. Through Barbara I met her husband Ronnie Knight - the gangster I aspired to be.

He always wore the best Armani suits, pristine white silk shirts, golf cufflinks, shiny shoes and the most expensive aftershave - pretty much the way I dress and smell now. I owe some of my stylish dress to Ronnie!

Mum met Babs when she was appearing in panto in Birmingham and they developed a friendship. While Babs performed in Babes in the Wood she stayed at our house in Sutton Coldfield for over a year.

She was a very flamboyant character. Whenever we went out for a meal, if she had not been noticed by anyone after about ten minutes, she would let them know she was there with that recognisable laugh. But she could be very bitchy, and very 'up herself'. Although she liked to draw attention to herself I liked her - even when she wasn't on stage, she managed to upstage me on occasions!

Ronnie was actually charged with murder in 1983. He was appearing at the Old Bailey in London, where dad organised half a million pounds bail. When the bail was paid Ronnie came back to our house and there was a huge party.

Naturally I managed to make a mint out of the situation - selling stories to newspapers. There were about 20-30 cameramen camping outside our house. I would tell the papers what they wanted to hear. I even told them I washed Ronnie's socks.

One night we all went out for a beautiful meal. During the night I bumped into Ronnie in the loo. He suggested, what would be really nice would be if I paid for the meal for everyone - and he shoved five big brown £50 notes into my hand.

"When the bill comes, make sure you get it," he said.

Just as I went to pay, the owner announced 'no charge'!

I couldn't get out of there quick enough with the £250.

In later life I was to meet up with Ronnie on numerous occasions in Marbella, but I have lost contact today. I had a lot of admiration for Ronnie and would love to look him up - and Babs.

That was such an interesting period of my life. But I was disappointed some years later to hear that Ronnie had been arrested again - for stealing a bag of prawns........

Here was an East End gangster convicted of robbery, then acquitted - then steals a bag of prawns.

Word got around that ours was the place to stay.

And before long, big names were turning up at our house.

Frankie Howerd was due to have Christmas dinner with us, but cancelled after slipping on ice and breaking his foot.

Freddie Starr was another guest at our house.

We went for dinner one night. During the evening Freddie asked me why I didn't tell my parents I was smoking.

"Why don't you just tell them?" he said.

But I didn't dare.

Anyway, later in the evening Freddie stood up as if to make a speech. He clinked the glass to get everyone's attention.

"Ladies and gentlemen, friends and family," he announced.

"One of the reasons we are here tonight is that John wants to confess ..."

I was mortified. Oh my God mum and dad are going to find out I smoke.

"He wants to confess that he is homosexual!" he added.

"No I don't!" I blurted. "I smoke!"

Surrounded by celebrities gave me the chance to take on my first role as an actor.

When Babs was living with us I was introduced to a guy called Tony Hardiman - famous for bringing the West End musical The Black and White Minstrels to TV.

I heard that Tony was auditioning for parts in the Tom Stoppard play The Real Inspector Hound. Gregory's Girl star Jonathan Sinclair was in the production and 'Dot Cotton' from Eastenders.

I thought if I play my cards right I could get a part in

this play. So I went along to the audition where there were about 300-400 budding actors. I almost felt guilty because there were all these hopefuls practising their Shakespearian verse and I just knew I would get the part.

But what I didn't realise was the role involved walking on the stage, moving a table, collapsing and lying under the table - and staying there totally still for 90 minutes as a corpse!

Of course I got the part.

The audience presumes that it's a dummy lying under the table for all that time. It's only when they 'find the body' and turn you over to see if you're alive that you get up at the end - and the audience realises you really have been keeping dead still for all that time.

So the 'dead guy' gets a standing ovation.

Central TV and the BBC did a news piece about the part at the time. It was billed as 'the job everyone is dying to do' and 'was it a dead end job?' etc.

Two of us were picked to share the role. We even did a Saturday matinee. We got £7 a night for our part.

My God it was fun!

But have you ever tried lying dead for 90 minutes?!

Still, at least I can say I have been an actor at the Alexandra Theatre in Birmingham.

Chapter 11
Hello, goodbye Isle of Man

It was around this time that another opportunity presented itself to me.

Dad opened a shop in the Isle of Man so I spent some time there living on the island.

I got a job - in a casino.

The job involved photographing people on holiday at the casino. Imagine - me taking pictures of people celebrating their win!

I would buy the film, take the photo, then the customers would give me £1 deposit. I was supposed to post the film and the deposit through the door of the camera shop. The next day the clients would come to a hotel where I would show them the developed photos.

I did take the deposits and do as I should for about a week. But one night I didn't post the money at the camera shop. Instead, I took the £30 and spent it on Black Jack and cards in the casino.

The upshot of it was I was arrested.

But as the past has already showed, I wasn't even a clever criminal.

I told the police I had posted the money through the

door. The police rightly asked why a thief would take the films as well as the money.

They had me there.

They also pointed out several other photographers had posted their films and deposits through the door. Wasn't it odd that only mine was missing?

Got me again on that one.

So of course it all came to light - and I left the Isle of Man.

But dad sent me back to run his shop.

I took care of the day-to-day business, but sensibly the manageress was given responsibility for the takings.

One night she went to bed early and left the takings in the shop.

I took a tenner so I could visit the casino. I only intended to take one tenner. If I won, I wouldn't need any more. But I had to go back to the shop to take some more money, and more, and more. In fact on my last journey back to the shop I emptied the place. I lost all the takings and the stock.

The manageress came down the next day and - well - needless to say, it was a horrendous time.

The old man arrived in the Isle of Man by plane.

You know, I used to watch Laurel and Hardy. And it reminded me of my own life. Here I go again. I could look at myself and say: "Well. That's another fine mess you've gotten me into ..."

The problem was it was easy money. Easy come, easy go.

Hard-earned money is a lot harder to spend I have since learnt.

Understandably I was thrown off the island unceremoniously by my dad.

Chapter 12
My Diane

I need to backtrack a little to tell you about the time I first met my gorgeous wife Diane.

My first memory of her was when I was about 17 and she was 15. She was the youngest sister of one of my mates Phil the Skin.

(You may remember, he was the one I offered the alibi to).

I used to call round his house in Four Oaks, Sutton Coldfield, where I met all his family.

My first memory of Diane was watching her putting her socks on, getting ready to go to school!

My mate's sister Diane - the person I was to spend the next 24 years with, at the time of writing.

I thought she was an absolute little sweetheart. She was a tiny dot, cute - so small I could put my arms right round her waist. She was like a little doll. Diane was also a bit of a rebel, with a cheeky face. I liked her the minute I saw her. But I have to admit I never thought I would marry her, because I was a real playboy.

You might not know it now, but I had highlighted blond hair and was a bit of a catch. I actually went out with a Miss Great Britain, Julie Duckworth (who was from Manchester) for a while. I met Julie at a trade show. She came sixth in the 1979-'80 Miss World competition. In fact she wore the earrings I bought her at that competition. We were together for about nine months.

But my life was not all about women. It was more about gambling, which left me little time for anything else.

Also, because of my gambling I could not afford women.

Di remembers one time when she and her friend spotted me in Birmingham one Saturday.

She says:

"He was walking through town with a sheepskin coat on. He was tanned. My mate said to me 'he's nice'.

I looked across the road and thought 'I know him'.

We bumped into each other a bit later. He had obviously been on holiday and asked me to go out with him, but I already had a boyfriend.

"Let's just go for a drink," he said.

We arranged to go for a drink. I agreed, thinking my boyfriend was working that night. But as it turned out he wasn't, so I rang John's home and left a message saying 'don't ring me because David is not working'."

All the secrecy caused loads of problems.

Mum thought I was going out with a married woman. It caused uproar in our house.

I remember going round to see Phil on Boxing Day - but really I'd gone to his house to see his sister. They were all enjoying a family Christmas, and Di sneaked out to have a cigarette with me in my car. I asked her if she would go out with me on New Year's Eve.

Di had split up with her boyfriend, but was seeing someone else - another of her brother's friends. Di appeared to agree, but she maintains nothing definite was planned.

Anyway New Year's Eve came round and she was getting ready to go out with her friends, when I rang her and said: "Where are you?"

She went out with her mates and left me on my own on New Year's Eve.

I went round to her house on New Year's Day where we enjoyed the leftover food, the turkey etc.

My first proper romantic date with Diane was at a snooker hall where I bought her a pint. I took her in my dad's van.

Diane still remembers I bought a pie on the way home and offered her a bite.

According to Di I said: "Do you want a bite?" Then I stuck the pie in her face.

It was not the most romantic of beginnings.

But within a few weeks she left home and we got a little one-room bedsit together on the Kingsbury Road, Erdington. It was fantastic. I taught Di to cook.

She would meet her mum at lunchtimes and her mum told her she could always come home.

I earned a bit of money here and there doing a bit for my dad, hustling money at snooker halls and gambling.

Her family hated me.

But I was not one to mess about as you've probably gathered.

Me and Diane got together in January, got engaged in February, she was pregnant in March, we married in August and had our first baby in December.

At last I had someone who knew and understood me, someone I could share my feelings with. This was a big change in my life.

But poor Diane got roped into my way of life.

Chapter 13
Nick

While we were living at the bedsit in Erdington I met a guy called Chris.

He was about 16 years old when I first met him - he had just left a local children's home and we became friends.

We used to have quite a laugh. We'd borrow cigarettes off each other, and we would play cards. He'd bring his cousin, who was still living at the children's home, round to our place. They were like little Artful Dodgers, but good solid people I thought - not afraid to get their hands dirty. And I could understand them.

Chris, who reminded me of a Walter Mitty character, was a frequent visitor.

On one occasion he asked us if we would help him. He needed to pick some furniture up which he'd left at his aunty's house he said. But it was about 60-70 miles away. I had a car, which I'd bought for £60.

I agreed to help, but cancelled a couple of times. Eventually it was arranged again and we set off about 9.30-10pm at night and drove down the M5. I just went where Chris directed me. I didn't know at the time, because it was dark, down country lanes; but I now know the place we visited was Ross on Wye.

Diane and Chris's cousin came with us too.

Chris was paying me £15 - but about £7 of that was used in petrol.

Anyway, we pulled up at the front of this cottage. Di and me sat in the car while Chris and his cousin got out. We were in good spirits, chuckling and laughing while we waited for them.

They came out carrying suitcases, a TV, pots and vases. It did strike me a bit odd that they were coming out of the back of the property, but I thought no more of it.

Then they started bringing guns out and put them with everything else in the boot of the car.

I thought: "Jesus Christ. This kid has an arsenal of weapons.

Then a camper van came up the drive and Chris started yelling: "Let's go! Let's go!"

The driver of the van stopped, looked then tried to block us in.

I thought: "What's going on?"

Chris just yelled: "Drive. It's my aunty. She's coming back!"

The drive was lined with tree stumps and I caught the exhaust as we made our getaway. I still just thought for some reason Chris's aunty didn't want him to take his stuff.

Anyway, the next day I went to see my sister (from my dad's 'other family') where I had arranged to mend the exhaust. Dad's first wife Mavis was there.

I arranged to give Mavis a lift back to her house on the Chester Road, Pype Hayes.

As we were driving towards her house a police Avenger

car drove past, and the cop was staring at my car. He stopped and put his blue lights on.

I put my foot down and shot down the Chester Road. It was only a short distance to where Mavis lived. There were three other police cars trying to block my route along the way.

Mavis said: "Oh look the road is blocked. There must have been an accident!"

She was totally oblivious, until the last few minutes that we were in fact in a high-speed chase.

I knew this was the end.

I still had the shotguns in the boot - and credit cards under the seat. I knew something was amiss.

It was only then the penny dropped about the night before.

Eventually I had no option but to stop near Mavis's home.

The police tried to handcuff Mavis, bless her. She was horrified - and so was I. It still saddens me that she had the shame and disgrace of having to walk into her house after my arrest.

I was arrested for burglary and taken to Erdington Police Station. I stayed there all day until 7pm. I'm ashamed to say Diane was also arrested outside our bedsit and put in a cell.

She did not have a clue what was going on - so she told the police where we had been the night before and exactly what happened.

The police showed me Diane's statement at about 5pm.

The game was up.

I was transferred from Birmingham to South Wales police and kept in custody for two days.

Di was bailed to appear before magistrates. I was remanded in custody. The police were telling Di I would get three years for this. One of the cops actually asked Di out for a date!

The whole experience was a massive shock.

I had met Di in the January. By May I was in custody in a prison in Bristol awaiting trial.

But it got worse.

It appeared on that night in Ross on Wye there were people in the cottage after all. They had been tied up in the house. So it wasn't even a burglary charge. It was armed robbery.

I was expecting to go down for three and a half to five years for something I absolutely knew nothing about.

It struck me as odd that while the world was carrying on I was in jail. True by Spandau Ballet was in the charts. Manchester United were playing Brighton in the FA Cup. Being a Man U fan for many years I had never missed a cup final!

Poor Di was horrified.

The bedsit was taken apart by the police and she moved back in with her parents. I wrote heartrending letters to her, while all the time literally expecting a 'Dear John' letter.

I was placed in a 'category B' prison for those who were 'highly dangerous and liable to escape'.

I already had convictions, so I thought it was impossible I would get away with this.

I adopted a kind of James Cagney 'I'm not bothered' attitude. But at night in my cell I wanted to sob my heart out. To this day, 25 years later I have nightmares about it.

Believe it or not I did meet some very nice people I there - some I am still in touch with now.

But there were some very scary people there. One guy John, was a serial killer. He had killed two members of his family and was serving a minimum 30 years.

My heart was wrenched further when Di came to visit me with my parents. Sitting in the surroundings of a prison she told me the news - she was pregnant. I thought I would not even see the child until it was about three years old, and that really hit home.

Yet I had done nothing wrong. I was guilty only of being gullible.

Chris was in the same cell as me - and he really lost it. He ended up on medication. Someone told him he had got to 'do bird'. So he sat chirping in the corner and on top of his bed.

I asked to be moved to another cell.

Then I shared with a muscle bound guy who seemed really nice. He told me he had turned to crime this last 12 months because he was heartbroken over the death of his mother who had been killed in a car crash. I felt really sorry for him.

But I did think it was a bit strange when he said he'd had a Mercedes put on the front lawn in memory of her. Turns out he had cut the brake pipes on the car and killed his mum ...

One night in my cell I witnessed a dangerous prisoner

being brought in. It took about ten police just to get him in.

One of Britain's most dangerous killers ended up in the cell next to me.

To make matters worse most of the men in the prison were Welsh. And I was accused of tying up and robbing one of their own. At that time there was a lot of anti Brummie/Welsh feeling.

During my stay in prison we played football, 11 a side on a five-a-side pitch. I went in for a tackle on a weedy little kid and rammed him up the wall, squashing him.

"Sorry mate," I said.

"Don't worry. I'll catch you later," he said pleasantly.

I though he meant he'd see me later …

Later in the day I was sitting on a bench and wondered why no-one would sit next to me. When I was in the dinner queue he kept staring at me, smiling and laughing.

He kept saying: "I won't forget that tackle!"

Turns out he was the equivalent of Hannibal Lecter! That's why no-one would dare sit anywhere near me.

Conditions at the prison were like something out of Victorian times. When I watch Ronnie Barker in Porridge it looks like luxury. We had a cup of tea out of bucket.

How people can say prison doesn't break people I don't know.

Yet again, my dad came to the rescue.

He employed the best barrister he could find. It was unusual in those days to have a barrister in a magistrates court. The magistrates actually wanted to send the case to Crown Court.

Eventually the case was heard.

Di was fined £60 and acquitted of burglary.

She was found guilty of allowing herself to be carried in the car.

Chris got probation as he was the youngest.

I had no option but to plead guilty to aiding and abetting, and driving the car.

I was given A SUSPENDED sentence for two years!

That drive back from Bristol to Birmingham was heaven. We had to pull in to a service station where I had a divine glass of milk!

From then on I knew my life would - must - change.

I had two great parents, a girlfriend and a child on the way.

It felt as if there was someone watching over me, a guardian angel, guiding me.

In a strange way I'm glad I went to prison and experienced it, though I'm not proud of it. It was a learning curve, and an experience I use when I'm talking to people. I've always tried to turn bad things into something positive.

When I look back now I think about what all this must have been like for Di's parents.

They had a daughter who was 18 and pregnant, and her guy had just come out of prison. He had even got their daughter a criminal conviction.

I wonder what I would do now if it were my daughter. How would I feel if she was mixed up with someone like that?

I reflect on it now. And people should take time to do

that about their own lives: how they got to where they are now and be thankful. Writing this book actually helps me when I think about those times.

So I went back to meet Di's mum with my tail between my legs. She gave me a stern talking to and I took it on the chin.

Dad gave me one of his shops to run in Alum Rock, so I was back where I started, with the Asian community. I was born in Alum Rock.

I was working in an area I knew well and felt I could actually start going somewhere. I realised I had gambled not only with cards, but with people's lives and emotions.

The gambling would stop here, I told myself.

I got myself a bright orange, carrot-coloured Comma van and set out to make my career in the second-hand business.

Same old story.

There was a fruit machine arcade a few doors away.

And before long I'd set up a card school at the back of my second-hand shop.

Any money I made at the shop was gambled away.

Chapter 14
Trying to Settle Down

So there I was in my little shop, with much of my life spent gambling with the Asians.

Me and Di had another little bed sit in Erdington. But despite everything that had happened, I would sneak out in the evenings to a mini casino playing on the roulette wheel or playing cards.

This was in the 1980s and what I earned at the shop was big money in those days.

But only a true gambler will understand how I could risk our entire savings. And only a true gambler will know the feeling when every penny has gone and you ask yourself: "How do I get more money?"

I couldn't get a proper full time job - that would interfere with gambling. All I could think of was get rich quick schemes.

By this time Di was five months pregnant, working for Birmingham City Council, an administration job to do with school meals.

Di knew the score. She knew this guy had made more money than most people make in a lifetime - but lost it.

But I had ambitions. I wanted to be like Ronnie with the Rolls Royce. That image played a big part in my life.

On the day of our wedding, which was in August, I

actually went to work at the shop in the morning. It was a Saturday so I could make quite a lot of money then. And the wedding wasn't until 3 o'clock.

When I arrived at work the neighbours had painted the shop up - with a picture of me wearing a top hat and pushing a pushchair.

On the picture was written "Hang on Di, I'll get 50p for this! Meaning I could even flog the top hat!"

I locked up the shop at 12 noon intending to go home and get ready for our big day. I jumped into our orange Commer van and drove down Alum Rock Road, which is quite a steep hill. I put my foot on the brakes - and nothing happened. I pumped the brakes frantically and they came back on for a few seconds, but I was going faster and faster.

All I could think was: "What a bloody year this has been. Now I'm going to get killed on my wedding day."

But somehow I got home in one piece and the wedding went ahead at Holy Trinity Church, Sutton Coldfield.

My half brother Colin was best man.

27 August 1983. It was a beautiful day after all - a very special day.

Di's family from Ireland turned up and gave us an envelope with cash in it.

I thought: "My God, I've got money again."

Our reception was held at the local library in Mere Green.

Di's family drank the bar dry.

She has lovely uncles, Michael and Joe, real down to earth people. It was nice to meet people who were warm and so genuinely glad for us.

Afterwards, me and Di went into Kentucky Fried Chicken restaurant in Erdington: Di in her wedding dress, me with my suit on. Then we went back to mum and dad's house where they said they had a surprise for us.

"Pack a case in the morning," they said.

The next day they drove us to Luton Airport. Di had never been out of the country so it was really exciting.

All the family waved us off. My sisters and half brother were there. There were about 14 of them altogether.

We were bound for Torremolenos.

And when we got on the plane the whole family had followed us. They had pretended to wave us off. They were all coming too!

We had a really great time out there.

After the honeymoon it was back to running the shop and the next lovely event in my life.

Baby Alexis Cheryl Ann was born on 23rd December, 6lb 6oz.

I was great friends with the snooker pro Alex Higgins at the time, so my daughter was named after him. I met Alex on the Isle of Man then met up with him again when Di was pregnant.

At this point in my life I realised I had to try to get my head round my situation. I had a wife and baby and I knew I had to be responsible.

So I got rid of the shop and took a job, working full time in Birmingham selling windows - and I became the top salesman. I knew deep down that sales was something I could succeed at and make a career out of.

Gambling was definitely something I had to get rid of.

I had a bunch of good lads round me and it was actually great to have friends who didn't gamble.

I did that job for about four to five months and became disillusioned with how the company was being run.

So I decided to set up my own company.

This was the start of what would be a series of calamitous adventures.

It was around this time that I indulged in another passion - banger racing.

When I was a child, my half sister Angela and her husband Dave took me to Hednesford Raceway in Staffordshire. I would watch the stock car drivers and think 'what a great life that would be'.

So I got myself an old car, stripped it down with Di's brother Graham and roll-caged it out.

I got number 162 - appropriate I thought, since I was born in 1962.

For my first race day we had to be at the track for 11am, but I had given no thought as to how I would get the car there - so I DROVE it there. It had no windows in it whatsoever.

How ridiculous can you be?

It even had PTO written on the side in large letters - a reference to the race itself when I hoped I wouldn't be turned over.

Anyway I got the car there and took part in the race. I lasted three laps and got absolutely battered. As soon as the flag went, everyone rammed me from every angle!

Yes, I was so proud walking through the crowd. I felt like James Hunt at the time - another chapter in my life where

I was trying to stand out in the crowd.

I did banger racing for about three months, taking part in racing at Birmingham Wheels. Di used to come and watch.

But it was a very expensive sport and I had no sponsorship - so it was time to hang up my helmet.

Even now when people tell me to slow down I say: “Don't worry, I used to be a racing driver!”

Chapter 15
Business ventures

I built up my own sales team in the Erdington windows business.

By this time Di was pregnant again, something I was pleased about. And she was pleased with me.

She thought I had settled down and would be the provider.

The sales company was doing well, so after a year me and Di bought a house in Four Oaks, Sutton Coldfield.

This was a major step for us. The house was in Slade Road and cost £28,000.

The first night we moved in, Ronnie (dad's first wife's brother) turned up in his Rolls Royce. I loved that, because all the neighbours could see.

About this time I invented a company based on the idea of a talking directory. I approached the Government Department of Trade and Industry for a £30,000 grant. The idea behind it was international rescue; i.e. if there was a flood or emergency people could phone up and a qualified, skilled rescue team would be sent out to them.

I had various meeting with Government officials and with an MP who was going to back the idea. I spent two years of time and energy on this idea - only for someone else to take it and turn it into Talking Pages. I never did take up the grant.

My head was always full of business ventures - even as child.

At the age of eight or ten I used to make nail files out of lollipop sticks and sell them to women.

As ever, I never missed a trick.

When I was a kid dad used to take me out selling potatoes. Dad and four other blokes sold them off the back of a big van. I used to do OK selling them too.

I remember one day a customer ordered a big bag of spuds for £1.50. The bag was bigger than me. It took me ten minutes to heave it down the drive - only to be told it was the wrong house!

But I learned something there.

The woman took pity on me and said: "Go on, I'll have them."

The other guys couldn't figure how I outsold everyone else.

The truth is - I often used to drag heavy sacks of spuds down people's drives, knowing that most of them would take pity on me and buy them anyway.

All the other lads got 25p a bag. I only got 10p. But one day, when I sold 17, dad decided it was time I should get paid full whack.

One day, when I was about ten, I hit on another idea.

I watched an old woman coming out of a shop. She was struggling with a bag of spuds.

I ran up to her and asked if I could give her a hand. She had potatoes for a week, but they were far too heavy for her.

So I hit on the idea of pre-packed potatoes, just 4 or 5lb. I set up a 'potato round'. As a ten-year-old I used to go round to pensioners, selling them just 2lb if they wanted.

I wanted to make money - but I still had a heart.

When we lived in Water Orton I used to go carol singing as a kid with my sisters.

Once we knocked on this old man's door after singing. He went off mooching about the house for change and looked a really sad figure.

I asked if he was OK. His name was Mr Newman and he told me his wife had died. He was about 70 or 80 and I just felt so sorry for him, especially as it was Christmas.

So I went singing for another one and a half hours. Instead of keeping the money I bought a box of Matchmakers and a card and wrote 'to the old man at No 6 - from the carol singer!'

I went back and delivered them too him. He was gobsmacked!

You see, I was always a wheeler-dealer. But I do have a nice side, even to this day. I still do charity fundraisers now. But more about that later.

The business ventures would get wilder, much wilder. And as ever there would be some highs and crushing lows along the way.

Chapter 16
Rock Bottom

My second child Matthew was born in May 1985.

The glass company closed down and my international rescue idea had collapsed.

So here I was with a wife, two kids and no job.

My only income was my unemployment money - which I was gambling away at the betting shop. The mortgage was £100 a month.

Di still thought everything was OK. I was about 23 at the time, very convincing and persuasive. But by June/July that year letters from the Building Society started to arrive. I buried my head in the sand.

By October we were to be evicted.

Dad could have bailed us out. But he had helped me so many times before that I think he wanted this to be a lesson in life.

Eventually I put Di in the picture.

We decided to get away from all the pressure for a while and show Di's family in Ireland the new baby.

So we picked up my unemployment pay which would just about enable us to get the ferry to Dublin with the two kids. The plan was to stay with Di's family for a short break. So we drove straight to Holyhead to get the night ferry.

I made sure Di was settled in the cabin with the kids then went for a cigarette. Walking round the ferry I spotted a blackjack table …

I couldn't even get my breath. It was as though someone had planted it there. I actually stepped backwards, as if in slow motion.

It was a table that took 25p and 50p bets - maximum bet a fiver. It was purely for entertainment, run by a woman sitting there with money in a shoebox.

I had our spending money with me. It was 11pm and we had a seven-hour journey.

So I decided: a maximum £2 bet, then I'd go back to the cabin.

The ferry was due to dock at 6am the next morning. At 5.45am I was still at the blackjack table when the woman said: "OK that's it."

Out of our precious £140 I had £1.50 left. I think if we weren't docking I would have felt like throwing myself overboard.

I got back to the cabin and Di said: "Where have you been?"

I didn't own up.

Our plan was to get a taxi from the dock to Di's gran's house. I hadn't even got the taxi fair.

"Wouldn't it be nice if we took the bus," I suggested.

And it was during that bus journey that I confessed. Poor Di was devastated.

When we arrived at her family's house she told her Uncle Michael, a painter and decorator.

He had a novel way for me to pay back the money.

Instead of enjoying a short break I had to work for him the whole weekend - then he'd give the money I'd earned to Di.

He had me painting horrible rooms in a convent on a boiling hot 'holy weekend'.

It certainly taught me a lesson and in the end we had a great weekend. Then it was back home.

Now it was October and we were going round family members assuring them we were OK.

To make matters worse Di was pregnant again. We went to Social Services to see if they could help with our housing predicament. Their answer was to take Di to a hostel to show her around. Husbands were not allowed there. It was for wives and children.

It was then that it hit home for Di. We had a lovely house in Four Oaks, and when she saw the squalid hostel she just cried.

When it came to the eviction I couldn't even afford to pay for a van to take our stuff away. All I had was a Mark II Cortina - not even a hatchback. Dad at least sent a van and put our furniture and some of our belongings into storage.

The bailiffs arrived one morning in October with a man from the Building Society. They put all our stuff on the lawn and gave us half an hour to get out with the two kids.

This time I wasn't wondering what the neighbours would think. I was just looking at our belongings on the lawn thinking 'where am I going to put all this?'. Thankfully the kids were too young to know what was going on.

There was no way Di was going to the hostel, so we went to my gran's, (my mum's mum) to stay the night.

There weren't many people willing to help us, and I felt people were kicking me down even further when I was at the bottom.

But my sister's husband's parents Connie and Ken were absolutely marvellous. Connie was a lovely lady, a regular babysitter for us. They only had a little flat in Erdington, but still made room for all of us to stay there for a week.

Then the council gave us a three-bedroomed flat in Valiant Croft, Castle Bromwich.

Let's just say it was known as 'Valium Croft'.

At least we had a home, and with my wheeling and dealing things started to pick up a little.

I even managed to get myself a flash pink Jaguar - registration ROB 3M - with the 3 turned the other way round!

Although I was on the dole I was gambling and playing snooker to make money. On a good day I could earn a bit.

Mum and dad as ever were wonderful and helped us decorate the flat.

Our first Christmas in 'Valium Croft' stands out in my memory. There was a lovely little family living in the flat below us - but they were so poor.

We went out to do our Christmas shopping and came back to the flat with a 'turkey'.

The man downstairs stopped us and asked: "Have you got a turkey?"

We told him we had and he called the kids to come and have a look.

"Kids! Come and see! This is what a turkey looks like!"

They were having processed turkey steaklets!!

If you threw a carcass out in Valium Croft, the kids would take it and play with it in the street. We lived there for nine months - and I knew this was not how I wanted my life to be.

Chapter 17
Business Adventures Drive Me Crazy

Clawing my way back up, we managed to buy a three-bed detached house in Walmley, Sutton Coldfield. The house, which cost £29,000, was near to both of our parents.

I had suffered shock and humiliation ending up in Valium Croft, so really knuckled down to get us out of there.

We became really settled, and my third child, Jonathan, was born there in 1987.

Alexis was four, and she started school nearby.

By this time I was working as a doorman at various bars in Sutton Coldfield. As often happens in my life, it was at one of those bars I met up with an old mate, Dave Felton.

When I first knew Dave he was a kid in a school uniform, just 16 years old - playing three-card brag in a pub. I was dealing the game, and I used to fix it so he would win. I remember he had a wonderful dad, a clever businessman called Brian, who I really looked up to and admired. He was a good, solid family man with a lovely wife and house in Sutton Coldfield. He worked so hard and had a great business, which he sold in 1987 for millions. Yet he was still 'one of the lads' - fun too.

I have found there are only so many good people in life. He was one I looked up to, and his son was to play a significant part in my life later.

At this period of my life, gambling was still a major part - but in those days you could not make it a career. So I was full of get rich quick ideas, and living off those.

One of my strangest included dogs.

Dogs always used to jump up and kiss me, and one day I had the thought that I had never smelt a dog with nice breath. So I began to research the ingredients for breath freshener used on human beings. A vet confirmed there was nothing in the ingredients that would harm a dog. So I came up with a recipe, and made barrels of blue-coloured dog breath freshener in the garage.

But it wasn't 100 per cent right. I needed something with a minty taste. Anyway I found a company that would bottle it, label it and wrap it in cases of 24. This was around the time when yuppies became the in word. So I called it 'Yuppy Dog Breath Freshener' and off I went selling it, cold-calling at shops. Word got around and the idea caused quite a stir in the press.

The stuff had to be squirted into the dog's mouth - and of course they hated it. Dogs started snapping at their owners, and one dog got a throat infection, so Trading Standards became involved. Needless to say I was sued and ended up with my first bankruptcy.

In those early days I've been a taxi driver, and I appeared on TV with a system on how to beat Black Jack. There have been some hilarious times.

Once, when I was in business with Alex 'the Doc' we

worked from a poxy little office in a huge building. Lorries were coming in and out of the building all day - so we pretended to customers we had this huge company and owned the whole building.

On another occasion me and Alec went to a factory which made freezers and cookers. The people who owned it were having a stock clearout. As we left, I noticed a lot of little boxes and asked what was in them.

"Enamel," we were told.

Well, white enamel to me meant the stuff that you had on your teeth, so I had a great business idea.

'Be like the Hollywood stars' my advertisement said - showing pictures of people with gleaming white teeth.

We just could not stop selling them. The enamel was flying out at £5 a time. When people ended up with burns and ulcers in their mouths from the toxic stuff that was the end of that business venture.

I worked on another venture with 'the Doc' called Dial a Clutch.

On one occasion we went with an estate agent to see a warehouse, an old paper mill that we were interested in opening as a clutch centre.

Inside the building there was a huge old bailing machine in the way. I phoned up a mate who told me it was worth a lot of money. I wasn't interested in the warehouse because it was too dear - but I wanted the bailing machine.

I offered to do the estate agent a favour. If he left me the keys, I'd get rid of the machine for a charge of £2,000.

Within a week, I'd been offered £6,000 for the machine - a cool profit of £8,000 for nothing.

Then I branched out on my own as King Clutch and made an absolute fortune, using different aliases and adding various 'extras' to people's bills.

I had five King Clutch centres across the Midlands and was making about £2,000-£3,000 a day - and gambling about £20,000 a week. I had huge wins, and huge losses - but overall lost. I would place bets of £40-50,000. I estimate I have gambled or turned over about £10 million easily.

After receiving numerous complaints, Trading Standards spent five years trying to prove I was 'the King' behind it all. They finally caught me by sending two actors with a court summons.

When I was interviewed I just repeated 'no comment, no comment' - but I knew the charges were so serious that I was going back inside.

There was only one way I could have avoided prison, and that was to be certified mentally ill and institutionalised.

So all the stress and trauma I had suffered in my life finally caught up with me.

I had read that patients would often go in on themselves and not speak. This is what happened to me. I would not speak to anyone for weeks. Eventually I saw five doctors who all thought 'something was not right'.

Well let's face it. Something was definitely not right with me.

Di was worried sick. She didn't know what to think of my condition.

So at 31 years old, the police accompanied me when I

agreed to be admitted to Highcroft Hospital in Erdington - a depressing Victorian building for the mentally ill.

While I was in the loony bin a doctor's report remarked that I had been found playing Monopoly with six other patients - for real money!

"He has a streak of competitiveness when asked to play scrabble," the report read.

They believed scrabble was very good for my communication skills. When I did speak it was to insist I'd play scrabble for a fiver a game.

So here I was in an institution with a fellow patient who said he'd invented the CD player and one who said she was Elvis's daughter.

Most of my time was spent lying on my bed, sleeping - and working out ways to get rid of the tablets, which I hid in my food after spitting them out. I would spit out the liquid medicine when the staff weren't looking.

In a scene reminiscent of The Fugitive, Trading Standards actually visited me in the institution. The man was told I was extremely ill, but insisted he had to see me.

I was sitting staring out of the window ...

He called: "Jon!"

I sat rocking, staring.

He called: "Mr Hewston!"

I sat rocking, staring, saying nothing. I would often rock all day long.

"You won't get away with this!" he shouted in absolute frustration.

There were two doctors and a nurse with him, who eventually insisted he left. But he continued yelling as he walked down the corridor.

We had had a cat and mouse game for five years. Now he couldn't believe he was in a place where he couldn't get at me.

Despite my illness I do remember turning round watching them leave. The Trading Standards guy was the only one still looking in my direction.

I remember winking at him …

When I got home life still wasn't exactly normal.

One day I was sitting at home watching Friday Night Live with the presenter Nicky Campbell on TV. It was a live interactive audience type show.

I was about 32 at the time, and at the end of the show they put out an appeal for well-known gamblers.

I suddenly thought: "I could go on TV!"

So I rang the show and told the programme makers: "I know of a gambler. His name is Jon Hewston and he's really big!"

I was gambling heavily at the time at Stackies Casino in Birmingham. I suggested they ring Stackies and ask about this Jon Hewston (not letting on it was me).

Anyway, I later got a call from the manager of Stackies.

He said: "We've had a TV company asking for you. They want you to attend the studios as a gambler."

The manager realised this was an ideal way to promote his casino, so he agreed it would be a great idea for me to go.

It turns out the show was really about gamblers who had a system. So when I rang the studio again (this time as Jon Hewston) they asked me if I had a system. Straight away I told them I had. In fact I had no system at all. I didn't have a clue.

The plan was to film me playing 'my system' of blackjack at the casino. Because of gaming laws at the time it was not allowed to transmit live from a casino, so they took the card table and dealer to the studios.

I was to be billed as this top pro' player with a system of how to beat the casino when in reality I was an amateur - with no system whatsoever.

I went to a studio in Nottingham with my friend Richard Chamberlain and my brother Colin. On the way they gave me advice on how to play. I did not even know how to play blackjack!

When we arrived there were pro' gamblers there including the great Alex Bird, well known horse racing expert Barney Curley, John McCririck and Wally Pira. (I later had the privilege of working with Wally's son in poker).

So the scene was set.

The producer introduced me as the pro' with the system. I was to play a JCB driver from Dudley - who was actually far more knowledgeable about the game than me.

The Stackies Casino general manager Martin Luigi had made it clear to me and the dealer, a woman, how important it was for me to win. It was in the interest of the casino that it appeared an enjoyable game that the house did not win.

We were given 1,000 chips each and left to play in the studio while a debate on gambling took place. Every now and then they would cut back to us to see how the 'intrepid

John' was doing.

After just 15 minutes I was losing £15,000 and had to ask the dealer to keep sending the chips back!

They asked me how I was doing on camera.

I looked them straight in the eye and said: "We're up."

The dealer looked at me as if to say 'you liar'!

I looked back at her as if to say 'ho ho! Remember what the manager said'!

The JCB driver, with no system whatsoever, was about £300 up.

I had no fear of being found out. I didn't care. I felt that if I could convince the TV audience and viewers that I had a system that worked, I may actually be able to find a system and have a book printed on how to beat blackjack.

I actually managed to pull the game off. I won back all the money I had lost and showed a profit of £800.

It was pure, desperate gambling.

As I was walking out of studio I heard a conversation between two producers. They were wondering where they could get two reformed criminals who were now successful businessmen for a future show.

Bingo! A light went on in my head!

Within 24 hours I was back on the phone to the production team stating 'I am your man!'

The following week, I was back in the same studio with the presenter Nicky Campbell. I was behind a black screen, blanked out, telling people all about my exploits. Needless to say, the TV crew were all very surprised to see me back!

I was so pleased with how it went I thought I'd see what

the next week's topic was.

It was child pregnancy ...

In the early 1990s I decided to make a career out of buying and selling goods on market stalls, buying job lots of various goods and selling them.

And I approached Jonny Morgan, a friend of my dad's, about setting up a shop selling ex-catalogue goods.

I walked into his office while he was talking to someone on the phone. I was also there to pick up £300 he owed me for some goods.

He told me to sit and wait while he was on the phone, so I was listening to his conversation. He was talking about greyhounds (of which I knew he had several) so I listened in hoping I could pick up some useful information.

I heard him say: "Yea. She's a great dog; I can get a good price for her."

When he put the phone down I asked: "What are you selling Jonny?"

"Jasmine, one of my greyhounds," he said. (For £300).

It did seem a coincidence at the time that he owed me £300. If only I had realised...........

So I agreed to have the greyhound instead of £300.

Then I called at the shop Beatties in Sutton Coldfield and bought myself a long grey coat (as worn by most racing pundits) and also bought a King Edward's cigar. Then I paraded into the house and announced that we were now the owners of a greyhound that was racing that evening at Norton Canes Dog Track in Staffordshire.

I had arranged to meet the trainer, someone called Dave, in the members' and owners' bar at the track to sign the paperwork for the dog and pay the kennel fees of £30.

Me and Di arrived at the track entrance where a guy said to me it was £1 to get in.

"We are owners," I said.

"It's still a pound in," he replied.

We paid then went into the private bar. I walked in dressed like (I thought) a million dollars. I asked everyone where Dave was and a woman pointed me in the direction of a drunken slob lying at the end of a bar. I introduced myself and the first thing he said was: "Have you got my £30 for the dog?"

So I paid him the £30 and the barmaid shouted over: "You can pay your bar tab now Dave!"

I mingled with the other owners trying to impress them - only to find that when I announced I was the owner of Jasmine people seemed to be looking at me strangely or ignoring me. There were several comments made and whispering going on which I didn't quite understand.

I went onto the track and approached one of the bookmakers and told him I was looking to wager a bet on Trap 5, Jasmine, in the second race.

"What are the odds?" I asked.

To my surprise he shouted at the top of his voice to the other bookmakers: "He wants to buy on Jasmine!"

"What are the odds?" I asked again.

"Whatever you want son!" came the reply.

Everyone around was laughing and I just could not understand why they were so amused.

The race came up so me and Di went to the ringside. The dogs were being led out in order: trap 1, 2, 3, 4 - then it went to 6.

No five.

We waited several minutes - only to see two men come out with chains, hauling this dog that I can only describe as looking like Pluto. It had great big massive paws and was like something out of a cartoon. Yet it had big leather straps on and a huge muzzle like the one used on Hannibal Lecter.

"It looks keen and mean," I thought.

They led Jasmine to the traps and we waited in anticipation.

The hare raced past me, the traps went up. We had a great position to watch the race.

The dogs were all bunched up and I was looking for the orange colour of trap five.

Jasmine was still inside the trap. Then she plodded out, leaving great big footprints in the sand, ran into the centre of the track and sat down.

By this time my swagger had gone.

We left the racecourse (hiding my face as we went past all the bookmakers).

I took the coat back to Beatties the next day and got my money back.

I never heard sight or sound of the dog again.

That was my only experience as a racing dog owner.

Chapter 18
Going downhill fast

I am now 32 years old, still living in Walmley.

Having spent another month in hospital I needed a new start.

My crazy life then took me to block paving. It was all the rage in the 1980s and '90s.

This is how my mind works - always thinking outside the box. I thought, with all this block paving going down everywhere, there must be a market for cleaning them. I found a company that produced a sealant and drove to London to meet an old man who had devised and patented a sealant for drives. I had done my research (via The Times newspaper).

This man was looking for people to help him market the product. So I arranged for two articulated lorries to take huge drums of his product to my 'storage depot' in Erdington.

The only thing was, the old man didn't realise my storage depot was a lock-up garage in a residential street. I told him I had a 'warehouse'.

But the stuff in the drums was highly toxic and explosive.

Imagine the residents' faces when hundreds and hundreds of drums bearing the scary skull and crossbones sign turned up in the street not far from where I lived.

They weren't the only ones to be horrified - I was.

I thought it was just a harmless sealant: not highly toxic, highly flammable and highly dangerous.

I had all the green anorak anti this and that protestors' brigade descend on me. I think I must have been one of the first to incite them. But what a dilemma. I had artics full of stuff and nowhere suitable to put it.

So I told the protestors there had been a mistake. The drums weren't toxic, I said. It was just floor cleaner. I even offered to clean their drives for them.

But in truth, the whole street could have blown up.

In the end I just abandoned the drums there and set up a company Imperial Block Paving.

I started to make good money out of this venture.

I got some vans on the road and had something like a little builder's yard. I advertised and travelled all over the Midlands - and things were going well.

Throughout this whole experience my main focus was to feed, clothe and educate my kids. But as ever, when all is well I have a tendency to take my foot off the gas.

I got involved with some unscrupulous people and some silly things, while at the same time taking cards and poker more seriously. But in the early days of playing poker I lost a lot of money.

I wasn't paying for products for my company. No-one was getting paid, so I ended up being sued.

Then I was asked to act as guarantor for a couple of friends who wanted to buy cars. I agreed. But the cars went missing and I had to take over the payments.

Then I started getting stuff on finance and selling them for a quick couple of grand - not one of my best ideas.

Before long I was in the shit again. I told lies and had numerous cars on finance. I cashed a £2,000 banker's draft, knowing it was fraudulent - and lost the money gambling anyway.

There were so many things I did wrong at this crazy time.

Suddenly the police were looking for me and the finance company people were coming round to my house. The bankruptcy courts were looming and I got done for drink driving.

I knew I was going down again.

I had dug myself into one huge hole and I could not get out. Di knew the situation too.

At this period in my life I was in trouble with the police and seemed to be constantly hiding from various situations.

So I tried, as far as I could, to keep a low profile.

But one day I got a call from a good friend John McGurk. He lived with his wife Linda and four kids and we had been friends for many years.

We often used to travel together to see Manchester United games. In fact I knew him even before I met Di.

John asked me where my boys were - because he said there was a TV crew in the area and they wanted to do a live feed to the studio about the Eric Cantona incident. Cantona had got into a fracas with one of the opposition team fans, jumped off the pitch and kicked him martial arts style. It had caused a big stir in the media. The boys, who were about seven and ten at the time, were Man U fans - so John thought it would be a good opportunity for them to go on TV.

So I agreed - and a satellite van turned up and interviewed the kids from Matt's bedroom, which was a shrine to Cantona. The kids were great. They talked about Cantona's outburst and went out live on TV, which created a lot of excitement.

The next day we had a phone call from Central TV in Birmingham asking if we could bring the kids along to the studio for the Friday Night Live show.

Because of my problems with the police, I didn't want to advertise my face, but I figured it was only the kids who would appear on screen in their Man U shirts, so I agreed to take them.

But when I got there the producers wanted me to sit in the audience with them. I told them I was involved with something and did not want to be seen. But they reassured me it would be OK. They would change my appearance a bit - put make up and glasses on me, and anyway I would not be shown. The focus would be on the boys, so I agreed.

There was a panel on the show, including a Man U player. There was an audience, wearing other teams' football shirts, and they were really slagging Cantona off. There were about 40 people there, but it turned out we were the only ones representing Man U.

Anyway, this guy poked me in the back.

"You're from the Midlands. You should've brought your kids up properly supporting a Midlands team," he said.

I looked at his shirt. He was a Derby County fan.

"Shut your mouth. And stop getting excited," I told him.

And in an obvious slur on his team's popularity I added: "Bet this is the biggest crowd you've ever been in!"

Before you knew it we were involved in a massive brawl - live on TV.

So, far from keeping a low profile, there I was, glasses flown off brawling in front of millions of people on a live TV show!

The producer's reaction was: "Marvellous. Just what we need for the show!"

Later on I went to the toilet with the lads. I was still in a very bad mood.

This guy came in and looked at the boys. And in a deep Irish accent he said: "Would that be a Man U shirt?"

"How clever are you?" I sniped - to which he gave me an evil stare. "Are you stupid or summat?"

Turns out he was about to take part in a debate with Alec McGuinness about two soldiers being killed.

It was Gerry Adams from the IRA!

I would like to take this opportunity to give a special mention to John McGurk, the guy who suggested the kids went on TV. We were great mates, our kids grew up together, and I taught John and his wife to play the card game Kalooki.

John had a great sense of humour and a great brain. In fact, he was one of the first people who said to me: "You should write a book."

He lived in Great Barr in Birmingham and ran a successful electrical testing business.

Unfortunately we fell out, which is very, very sad.

But I often think about him. We had a bust-up, something to do with his son working with my son Matthew in the Cayman Islands. We booked all the flights then his son didn't go.

Then we were supposed to travel to a football match, but I didn't go. Anyway, we used to be best of friends and seemed to be on the same wavelength. I just want him to know I miss talking to him.

Back in the real world I developed symptoms, which oddly enough I had witnessed when I was in the mental institution.

I told doctors there were people in cloaks looking for me - a kind of paranoia experience.

I ended up back in the mental home for another month.

At least it gave me a breathing space to sit and think and get my head right.

And I had enough about me to tell the staff I had changed my religion to being a Muslim, so I could get curry while I was in the loony bin.

Now I think this was all part of the building process that put me where I am today. It was while I was in the institution that I spotted an ad' in the Daily Mirror.

'Earn thousands. Live and work in the sun' it said.

It was to do with timeshare selling at holiday resorts in Majorca.

"That's it!" I thought - and cut out the ad'.

When I had a day out of hospital I rang up to enquire.

Di was all for it.

But I had no money to set me up there.

Di had the family allowance and a bit of money she'd

earned hairdressing. That was all we had in the world - and despite everything she trusted me and gave me the money.

Di got me there.

Chapter 19
This is the life - and near death

So off I went to Majorca in May.

I told myself: "This is your last chance."

I promised Di I would work as hard as I could so she and the kids could join me on her birthday, 10th July, in the summer holidays.

For the first four weeks I was lonely, struggling, and lost two stones in weight. I would ring home desperately upset saying I wanted to come home, but Di would say: "There's nothing here for you. You have to make this work."

I was living in a basic apartment and felt I could not make this work.

But by June I was managing to get my feet under the table.

Di and the kids came over to join me and we lived in just a small place, but I was much happier because they were with me. Di, my rock, was there.

I used my wife and kids to help me selling timeshare. I would speak proudly of them and show their pictures to clients. I had quite a rapport with people.

Gradually things turned around - and I made thousands.

I became the best salesman, a legend. My wages became phenomenal.

We were in Majorca from 1995-1999 and we lived like kings.

Our children aged eight, 10 and 12, were educated at private school on the island.

Di was amazing. She drove for four hours every day Monday to Friday to take the kids to their school and pick them up.

It was important to me for the kids to have a stable life.

We had the best property, the best cars, the best clothes and we went to the best restaurants. Life was great. It was a good time in my life.

I was selling the dream to customers and they were happy.

I met some great characters and lovely people.

One of them was British heavyweight boxer Alan Logsdon. He was head of security for our company - a real bouncer-type.

I used to spar and train with him and we remained good friends after I left Majorca. He would visit me at my home back in England.

Sadly, at the time of writing Alan died suddenly from a heart attack. He was only in his late thirties - one of the fittest men I ever met.

Although a hard man physically, he was a true gentleman.

I had my own brush with death while I was in Majorca.

I remember the date exactly - July 9th - a Sunday afternoon. It was Di's birthday the next day, so we decided to go for a drive with the kids.

We pulled up at a go-kart track. My son Jonathan would have been about 11 years old at the time.

Jonathan, who wasn't one to have a sixth sense as far as I knew, said something very strange.

"I don't want dad to go on a go-kart. Something is going to happen," he said. "There is going to be an accident."

The kids went off on the rental go-karts - then I spotted a real, powerful professional kart and asked the guy if I could have a go.

He told me I needed a proper licence to drive one of those, so I told him I had one. (Well, I did have a driving licence, and I had raced bangers).

"I'll be OK," I said.

So off I went on the track.

There was another guy on the track in a powerful kart - and I noticed he was going much faster than me.

Anyway, we started to race.

I was actually catching him up when we came to a straight section of the track, so I really put my foot down. I was doing about 120 mph. Without brakes I turned the kart so quickly it rolled and rolled and rolled.

All I remember thinking was 'shit'.

I still have nightmares about that roll to this day.

I was also thinking: "This is not the right time to die!"

It was then I had one of the most extraordinary experiences of my life- a kind of out of body experience.

I was lying on the racetrack and I can still remember drifting. Then I couldn't hear anything around me. I was lying on my side, looking ahead.

I could see photographs in white fluffy clouds - faces - coming in and out. But the extraordinary thing was one of the photos was an old neighbour Mr Atkins, a shopkeeper who used to look after me. Even now I find the experience hard to explain.

I went into a state of tranquillity and did not care what was going on. And I remembered the experience vividly days after the accident.

As I lay on the track my sons came running screaming towards me. Despite my predicament, all I could think of was how embarrassing it all was. I tried to get up, but couldn't. That's when you know you're really in trouble.

I was aware I was breathing really fast, and tried to stop myself but couldn't.

I must have been in shock. But I learned later that my lung had collapsed and I was actually fighting for air. I can see now how people die in accidents, when there isn't any visible mark on them.

I had severe internal injuries and was taken to a private hospital as I had insurance. I had internal bleeding, a ruptured right lung, my rib cage had collapsed, my shoulder blade was dislocated and the tips of my fingers were ripped off.

One of the doctors warned my family: "He might not make the night."

Work colleagues came to visit me in hospital - took one look at the state of me and walked out again. I could tell by the look on people's faces that I was in trouble. I had been racing, not in leathers, but in a pair of shorts. I had shattered my body.

I was more or less 'out of it' for 11 days.

I owe everything to the German doctor who treated me, and the nurses who cared for me. They were fantastic. But this was typical of the way my life had gone till now. There were two instances in the hospital, which nearly shocked me to death.

One was when I found out I was in the wrong hospital, so my insurance would not cover the £10,000 bill.

The other shock came after two days in intensive care.

My mum and dad came in with my sister Sami. They got quite emotional seeing me all wired up. There were two young women with them, about in their late 30s.

"I have somebody to introduce you to," mum said.

"These are your long-lost twin sisters!"

What a fuckin' shock.

What long-lost twin sisters?

I just thought: "Oh my God - more people I haven't met."

I swear that nearly killed me.

These were two girls I was not aware of from my mum's first marriage.

When she set up home with my dad he agreed to take on my older sister Stephanie, but not the twins.

One of my new sisters turned out to be an intensive care nurse! She told all my family what was going on and what the staff were doing for me.

The kids in our family all had 'S or J' names: Jon, and sisters Sammy and Stephanie. The twins were no exception - Suzanne and Janine.

The twins stayed for a short while then disappeared

from my life again. I think my parents thought I was going to die, so they'd better let them meet me. They only spent about three days with me, but they never met the real me because I was too emotional to express myself.

They did not see the jovial person who enjoys a laugh.

The twins are just another chapter in my bizarre family life.

We didn't keep in touch after that strange meeting, so didn't build up any relationship.

I don't know to this day where they grew up. All I know is they were living in Skegness when I was in Majorca.

My mother had a strange upbringing. There was some story about her meeting her half brother after 46 years - when he moved into the same street!

Chapter 20
Onwards and upwards

I was allowed out of hospital after 11 days.

I was still very ill, but there was no more they could do on a ward than what I could do at home. I was having physio on my lungs to try and remove the blood.

I was worried sick. The hospital bill ran into tens of thousands. I was in a foreign country and not able to work and had to pay the kids' private school fees. But the owner of the company I had worked for paid the hospital bill for me.

I managed to repay him by pulling off a big deal about a month after leaving hospital - even while I was still on crutches.

As luck would have it I bumped into a guy with his two sons. We got talking because they were Manchester United fans.

Turns out he was looking for a property. I was supposed to be convalescing, but I pulled off one of the biggest deals time-share ever had. The deal was worth £160,000 and I earned over £30,000 on it.

The company owner was so pleased he gave me a £5,000 bonus. In the end I made about £37,000 on that one deal alone.

Selling time-share was a real fun-filled job. It involved

walking people round, showing them the property. Then they would be wined and dined in the evening.

Often the contract would be signed while they were drunk, and I had many an interesting evening.

I worked on average about 90 hours a week, but there was plenty of money to be earned.

And because of my natural charm I was very successful!

Around this time I had been playing backgammon on line for about six to eight months. I came up with the idea then of an online poker site. People were experimenting with it, but it hadn't been done properly. I had the image of online poker years before it came of age.

I knew there would be a big demand because of the enjoyment I get out of it. But even I never realised it would be as big as it is today.

While I was in Majorca I noticed kids on the street approaching people with scratch cards - the 'touts' as the locals know them. They would hold morning meetings in a bar, drinking tea and coffee.

So I started looking from outside the box into the box as usual. I thought there could be some money to be made here.

My next venture was to open a bar and betting shop combined on the island. A bar came up to rent near where we lived, so I got a lease on it. I opened it as an English bar, but a bar where you could watch the racing channel inside.

So, I needed a satellite dish.

This is another typical example of how my life goes.

I was told the only dish to pick up the racing channel

would be an industrial one, so that's what I ordered from a guy I knew. He said he'd deliver it in a week or so.

Ever impatient, I asked him why he just couldn't fetch it in the car.

What a laugh.

When it finally arrived - it was so big it was delivered by low loader. It was the biggest satellite dish I had ever seen - about 30ft, like something you would expect at GCHQ tracking missions to Mars.

When I saw it coming I thought: "What the hell is that?"

There it was being fitted in a field next to my bar.

Within 24 hours I was broadcasting British racing to a Spanish bar, which was never heard of then.

The betting business opened up and it really attracted the locals. I employed a British bookie and his girlfriend.

One day I was taking the bets when a young guy in his 30s came in. He sat with a lager and I watched him send his wife and kids down to the beach. It was a Saturday morning and they had just arrived. He looked joyful, with that look you get when you're on holiday.

By 4pm I was looking at a different persona. The guy was sweating, gripping his tickets and obviously in a state. Being a gambler, I knew exactly what he'd done. It brought back memories of me on that boat trip to Ireland.

"Alright mate?" I said. "I'm not being rude, but what have you done?"

"I've done everything," he replied.

The guy was genuine. He had lost £700 - the family's entire holiday money.

So I gave it him back.

I wondered whether I was doing the right thing, but I want people like him to learn from the mistakes I made. I'm a great believer in what goes round comes round.

His expression was as if he had asked someone to grant him a wish.

"Come and have a drink," I said. "But you're banned from gambling here."

Today gambling is a major problem. I predicted it would be. But we're now only seeing the tip of the iceberg because people can get so much credit.

And as my dad said to me: "You never see a poor bookie."

I have to say it genuinely hurt to take people's money off them. Even now I have to say to myself: "If I don't take it someone else will."

Looking back, timeshare was a tough business to be in because it can be very cutthroat. But I will never regret going to Majorca. To live in the sun and bring up your children somewhere where they can swim every day is wonderful. We were cocooned there, with no crime - and I made a lot of money.

It was while we were in Majorca that I went with my son Matthew to see the cup final Manchester United v Bayern Munich. This was the highlight of my life. To stand on the terraces and watch Teddy Sherringham score a goal was great.

I spent five years living in Majorca and it felt like my second home. But Di had this urge to go home.

The kids would be coming up to their secondary education and we wanted them to be at private school in

England.

Di was also worried about her dad because he had a bad shoulder and a cough.

So we made some enquiries and found out about Lyncroft House, a private school with a good reputation in Cannock, Staffordshire. So we rented a house in the best part of the town, Shoal Hill and moved back to England.

Chapter 21
The hardest words

So there we were in Cannock in 1999 and I had to earn money.

Because I knew about timeshare I set up a company in the front room of the house buying and selling time-share properties abroad.

After 12-18 months I had 30-40 staff, so I rented an office in the town. It was a lucrative business and I did that for about two years.

Because of my background the police had a hard time accepting everything was above board. I would have my office raided, but officials could never find anything untoward.

But I wasn't destined to stay in the office. We had only been back in England for about two or three weeks when Di's dad got his diagnosis. He had lung cancer.

He died within about 12 weeks of us coming home.

As I write this book I remember the many years I spent not talking to Di's dad. But in the final weeks of his life I believe he accepted me. It was a time when we were able to make amends. We spent time looking back at old photos.

Di's dad came to live at our house in Cannock for the couple of weeks before he died.

It was a very traumatic time, and one of the hardest things I have ever had to do in my life was telling Di that he had gone.

Her dad was a true gentleman.

There were often times when we didn't see eye to eye, but he was the straightest, most honest man you could wish to meet.

He was the only person I knew who never had a red bill. When I was first with Di she never even knew what a red bill was. I can even remember her as a kid walking to the Post Office carrying a blue bill.

During this time in my life I was under a lot of stress, which may account for the following incident.

I was upstairs at home, when I started to feel hot and sweaty and there was a pounding in my chest. Di looked at my pale complexion and decided there and then I needed to go to hospital. She took me to Cannock Hospital straight away where I was placed on a heart monitor. Staff found I had an irregular heart beat and my blood pressure was high so they phoned for an ambulance and had me rushed to Staffordshire General Hospital in Stafford, while I had to use a special spray on my tongue.

So there I was again - in an ambulance yet again. But this was altogether a different experience. All I could think of was 'this is it'.

I was put onto a side ward and underwent various tests. A doctor then announced to me: "You've had a heart attack."

But he said the attack would have been in the last three to four years.

I sat there absolutely stunned.

Next I was placed on the coronary care unit where I had further tests and was examined by specialists. I was placed on a treadmill and had to run while wired up to machines.

They discovered I did have an unusual heart beat. They explained that a heartbeat has peaks and troughs. Where mine should have peaked, it troughed!

About a week before this incident I hadn't been well. I had been mowing the lawn at home when I had an asthma attack.

Anyway, back at the hospital I was to receive even worse news. Because of the test results they realised I had been misdiagnosed. I had not had a heart attack at all.

Why was this even worse news? I was insured for £250,000 in the event of a heart attack, that's why.

So instead of being elated I was so fucking down. Where most people would have been over the moon I was so depressed! I felt so down on my luck again I nearly did have a heart attack.

Anyway, as a result of this fiasco I went on a low fat diet and lost two stones and started to look after myself. I also realised smoking was playing a big part in my health problems. I had been smoking since I was a child.

But it wasn't until four years later that I was able to kick that habit.

Chapter 22
Big Games, Big Names

Suddenly there was an explosion in the world of poker.

TV's Channel 4 launched late night poker, which took the game from 20-30 people in a room to nationwide TV.

I was invited to play on one of the big matches. But the entrance fee alone was £3,000, which I couldn't raise. I turned it down, but agreed to put a friend of mine in - Peter Costa, who I rate as one of the best players in the country.

But he entered himself - and went on to win £60,000.

If I could have shared his entrance fee I would have won a 50/50 share.

Televised poker was the big turning point - the realisation what I was destined to do.

That weekend I went to the Rainbow Casino in Birmingham with Di. I had been going there since I was 15 years old.

There were some great characters there, including the general manager Duncan Savage who had known me since I was a child. It was a very friendly place with a great atmosphere. Run by a wealthy family, the Morell brothers, It became the lion's den of cards games - the 'Holy Grail' of poker. One of the guys who visited there was Charlie Kray, one of the Kray brothers.

World champions played there over the years. Sadly the club doesn't do poker any more.

This Saturday night I sat down with £2,000-£3,000 in my pocket - with willing sharks ready to take my money.

That night I had a drink, though I have never been much of a drinker. It was a really big game ahead.

Joining the table was the man who was to become my future friend and mentor, Micky Wernick - one of the most recognised poker players in the world. I had seen him in some really big games.

I had this particular hand. I raised.

He raised me. I raised. He raised.

I put all my money into this hand.

The pot was that big they had to bring casino staff to count on the table.

Mickey looked me in the eyes.

I looked Mickey in the eyes, showing no fear.

I can always remember what he said to me.

"You're showing no fear - young buck!"

I said: "I have got no fear."

The cards were shown.

We both had the same hand!

It was just one of the greatest moments.

We both won about £18-19,000.

After that game we became great friends and he took me under his wing. He was in his mid to late 50s; I was 37 at the time.

Mickey is a really great guy who has taught me a lot about the game. He really should write a book about poker. That would certainly be a best seller.

We started to travel everywhere together, anywhere where we could play poker. I seemed to be in my own little world: more interested in where I was going, than were poker was going, even though I could see the potential.

By 2001 I had bought our house in Cannock. Me and Mickey drove from the Midlands to London for the European Classic at the Victoria Casino. We had been lucky enough to get the last two seats in the game.

I picked Mickey up at 2.30pm, leaving plenty of time for the start of the game which was 7.30pm. But we were delayed and eventually set off at 4.30pm - then hit a massive traffic jam on the M1. Everything was going wrong.

Even when we got to London there were diversions and road works. The rules are, if you are not there by 7.30pm you are not allowed to play. At 7.25pm we were still stuck in traffic in the centre of London.

This is where my motor racing days came flooding back.

I did a handbrake turn, went through every red light and the wrong way down one-way streets - arriving at the casino at 7.29pm!

The evening had not started well.

But I was still in determined mood - if only because after all the hassle of getting there, the last thing I wanted was to be knocked out at 9pm and having to hang around waiting for Mickey until four in the morning.

But the biggest thing was - I had seen the trophy on our way in: this beautiful, big trophy. I imagined that trophy in my house. All I could think about was that trophy, even more that the prize money. I just desperately wanted to be a champion.

But my chips were going down and I had low stack. And the thought of having to hang around for hours gave me extra determination.

A personal friend of mine, known as the Devil Fish in poker circles, patted me on the back.

"How are you doing?" he asked.

"I'm nearly out," I replied.

He let me borrow £100 and someone else gave me a loan, so I got an add-on with the chips and started to build a healthy stack.

Every time Mickey looked at me I seemed to be saying congratulations to someone and shaking their hand. I was winning. From an original 168 players we were down to about 60.

Me and Mickey were still in. So was the Dutch player Marcel Luske - recognised as the one who puts sunglasses upside down on his head.

The line-up of the calibre of players was phenomenal. Although they were not celebrities then, it included some of the best players in the business today, household names such as the world class Barney Boatman and Joe Beavers.

We had to stay the night when the game went over to the following day. Me and Mickey scraped some money together and shared a room at the Metropole Hotel. I just couldn't sleep. I was pacing up and down, and I kept waking Mickey up saying: "What shall I do?"

"You can win it. Shut the fuck up and go to sleep," was the reply.

There was total prize money of £80,000, first prize being

£37,000 - and I was one of the chip leaders.

We were down to 60 of the best players in the world.

In the morning I had a meeting with Joe Beavers, Simon Trumper, Ram Vaswani and the Boatman brothers . They were intending forming a group of players called the Hendon Mob, and I was interested in managing them.

We had our meeting, but left with nothing set in stone.

They became multi millionaires ...

At the time poker sites were just about appearing online, but the interest was not on a grand scale, and I had no knowledge of how they would be run.

Play resumed at 2pm, and after three hours I was playing in a very aggressive style.

The table dwindled down to nine of us, which included Mickey, me, Marcel Lusk, Joe Beavers and the great Bambos (a London hotelier and well-known, successful player).

There was now a crowd of about 30-40 people watching.

This is where my acting career came into its own! I started to play to the crowd, and I was absolutely loving it.

We were now down to five players. Mickey was still in.

Then Mickey was knocked out - but he stood behind the observation rail, cursing me when I made mistakes and cheering everything I did right.

Then we were down to three: me, Bambos and Tim Flanders (whose wife was to beat me when I came second in the World Open).

Eventually the other two gave in.

I was the champion.

I took the trophy and £27,000.

When I was being presented with the trophy I looked across and saw Mickey with a tear in his eye!

I gave £2,500 to Mickey - and £2,500 'investment money' to the Devil Fish.

I felt invincible - and the trophy sits proudly in my house as a reminder of that day. I also loaned the trophy for a few weeks so it could go on display at the Grosvenor Casino, Walsall, in the West Midlands. After that high point I continued travelling the country with Mickey. We were inseparable.

I would sponsor Mickey, who was an absolute legend at this point, a great, strong player, competing against billionaires playing in Las Vegas. Mickey was the most well-known British poker player in America.

I knew I was good, but was still playing in the same circles. You would see the same faces at each event. You knew who would be there even before you arrived. I developed as a fearless, very aggressive player - because I had no fear of losing.

My business was now taking back seat - and I would take money out of the business for entry fees to poker tournaments. Sometimes it cost £2,000-£4,000 to enter me and Mickey - and we could come back with nothing.

When I was 38-39, we travelled across Europe: to Holland, Ireland, Vienna, playing against the best.

Still there was not much poker on TV. Still it was the same faces doing the same circuit. I was winning small tournaments - but the sparkle of the bright lights was yet to come.

Di still wanted me to get 'a proper job' at this point.

We played regularly at the Rainbow, which sadly is now closed. I don't understand why.

In 2001, when I was 39, me and Mickey took the plunge and went to Vegas. I saved about £19,000 (around $30,000). I had been to Vegas before, but only passing through as part of a holiday.

A family friend of over 30 years, Mark 'Snapper' Sullivan, came with us on the trip. In his late 40s, he was a friend of both my dad and Mickey. Incidentally my dad used to play cards with Mark's mum.

Mark was a great laugh, and great company, so I paid for him to go with us.

We all met at the airport. Although we were off to Vegas we didn't have enough money to play in the main poker event at Binion's Casino, which cost $10,000 each to enter. But I desperately wanted to play in the world championship.

We had to change planes at Cincinnati airport and had to clear customs. I was just so excited about being in the USA. I had read on the plane that you should only take $10,000 into the country, but I had $30,000.

"Why have you got so much money?" they asked.

"I'm off to Vegas. What do you expect?" I said.

In contrast Snapper had £1.80! He did have a fiver, but bought 20 cigarettes and a newspaper. So customs were saying he couldn't come in.

"Jonny! Tell him you've got my money!" he pleaded.

I had to sign to say I would take good care of him and we were allowed to carry on to Vegas.

We arrived at 8pm in a limousine and stepped out into

the bright lights. I just thought 'Oh my God' - and ran to the first poker table. I didn't even check into the hotel or unpack.

Even when I eventually checked in, I threw everything into my room and went straight back down to the poker table - and won £4,500 playing blackjack.

The casino hosts fetched whatever we wanted. By 3am I ran to Mickey's room to tell him I had won thousands. That was just the first night.

I then entered the Super Satellite, which is a tournament to win a seat in the main event. It was $200 to enter and there were about 180 entrants. There were about eight places left.

I won a seat for the main event. So did Johnny Morgan from Wolverhampton in the West Midlands. It was just tremendous.

I was so ecstatic I went straight to the airport, got on a plane back to England to tell Diane, then flew back to Vegas two days later - taking her with me! How I didn't kill myself with jet lag and deep vein thrombosis I don't know.

Snapper was given about $200-$300 'walk about' money and he left before the main event - with about eight bags of shopping.

"Never again," he told someone. "I had to ask for everything!"

While I was in the USA I met Mike Sexton a small-time poker player who was promoting a poker site there called Poker Stars. If I had used my loaf there were a lot of things I could have got involved in.

The World Series only came about because Benny

Binion got together with ten guys who wanted to see who was the best in the USA.

The first tournament in the 1970s had just 11 players. In the 2006 World Series there were 8,800!

Binion's Casino really was the home of poker where you could play for $5-10. It started when Benny Binion bought the Eldorado Club and Apache Hotel in 1951, reopening them as Binion's. It was the first casino to have carpeting and the entire Binion family was involved. But the World Series has now been taken away from there.

The birth of poker carries a lot of nostalgia.

Mike Sexton was a large gentleman and larger than life. I met him during that trip to Vegas and he asked me about the popularity of poker in England and whether it would work on TV. I told him we had a show called Late Night Poker.

He said he was thinking of doing something similar in the States.

And he did. He brought poker onto mainstream TV.

I actually sat next to Mike again at a function last year.

While I was in the States I met Benny Binion's daughter and grandson.

I also met Johnny Chan who starred with Matt Damon in the poker movie Rounders.

I was still quite young to be playing poker. I was only in my late thirties, but many of the players were in their 60s. I have seen big corporations take over as poker has become a multi billion pound business.

But it never used to be like this. We used to eat together then play cards. Now it's gone fuckin' crazy. More and more people are being drawn towards poker - and I'm not sure whether that's a good thing or not.

The World Series is played in a big function room at the Vegas casino, where friends and family are allowed to watch.

By 2002 you could see the popularity of poker growing. It was as if there was an explosion - and all because the Internet got involved. Ladbrokes created a poker site and it was as if overnight poker turned into a phenomena.

Chapter 23
Poker online

A new breed of player has been born - those playing on line.

Gone are the stone-faced poker players of old. Now you don't even see their faces.

They are the Internet kids, who play the game fast and think they're the bees' knees with their l.o.l. language.

I like to pick up on the body language of poker players. It's great to watch someone in a sweat, see the vein in the player's neck pulsating, the neck bulging, and watch them swallow. Online you can't see any of that.

The Internet kids even wear sunglasses so you can't see their eyes. I believe they can't even make a decision unless they have a mouse in their hand.

To some extent TV and the Internet has ruined the game.

TV doesn't show the perfect poker player, though it shows people risking the whole tournament with total bluffs, humiliating others.

To me, the perfect game of poker is where you have two people who have been playing for over ten years. They know and respect the moves and could create new ones.

Feeling the Internet sites were not the way to play, I decided to create my own.

Back in Britain it was noticeable that more tournaments were taking place all over the country and websites were starting to grow.

Within poker circles by now I was well in the rankings, in the UK and Europe. In 2002 I was in the top ten players in Europe, but poker still wasn't on TV all that much.

Then it all changed in 2003.

The popularity of TV poker meant my phone started to ring. I had invitations to many events - then bigger and bigger events.

My name was coined about this time when I walked into a tournament and someone called out 'Jonny Texas'.

Poker players have fun with their names. Dave Ulliott, from Hull, one of the great poker players became Devilfish.

Micky Wernick became The Worm - because every time you chop him up he keeps coming back! (Mickey always calls me Tex).

In 2003 the bottom fell out of timeshare, so by 2004 I had set up a business buying Argos clearance and opened three or four shops across the Midlands. (My dad had made quite a lot of money dealing with ex-catalogue stuff, so I knew about the business).

It was around this time that an opportunity arose to work in the Caribbean where timeshare was being re-launched.

I figured it wasn't far from the USA, so I would easily be able to fly there to play poker.

We rented a house at Grande Cayman in the Caribbean.

The boys Matthew and Jonathan came with us, but Alexis stayed in England.

We had a lovely home, went swimming every day, had barbecues by the pool, the wages were flowing in and I worked at this beautiful resort, travelling back to England every month.

I often think of a story I heard while I was in the Caribbean. It kind of sums up life for me. It goes something like this:

There was a man on a beach with a fishing line round his toe. Every now and then his toe would move slightly and he would pull a fish in. Someone asked him if he ever thought about selling his fish, so he could buy himself a rod.

"What would I do then?" he asked.

"You could buy a boat," came the reply. "You could catch more fish and sell them from shops."

"What would I do then?" he asked.

"You could buy a lorry, then lots of lorries to transport the fish."

"What would I do then?"

"You could buy a fleet of boats and be a multi millionaire."

"What would I do then?"

"You could lie on the beach and sunbathe all day."

There had not been a hurricane in the Caribbean for 40 years - but one hit when we were there in 2004 and it absolutely wrecked the island, including our home and the place where I worked.

Because of the storms - and because we were starting to

suffer from 'island fever' we made a decision to return to England. The island was so small that it could drive you crazy. If you wanted to go for a drive in the car you could only go for about an hour and you would be at the coast again on the other side. I still had a shop and business in the UK, so we made the decision to come home.

Back home I bumped into an old mate Dave Felton again.

We talked about poker and I told him I was going to enter the World Series. We talked about how expensive it was to get into big events and how poker had suddenly really taken off.

Dave told me his dad had been taken ill and offered me the opportunity to go and see him at Good Hope Hospital, Sutton Coldfield.

When you see someone who is strong in life, someone you admire struck down with an illness it makes you realise what life is about. It doesn't matter who you are or what you have got, it can all be taken away at any time.

Dave's dad being taken ill, suffering with cancer, came as a great shock to me. When he was hospitalised I went to visit him two or three times and it was easy to see he was not a well man. It was hard to see him like that in hospital, and I will always remember what a great guy he was, a true gentleman. He was a down to earth man in an NHS hospital. When he passed away it was a very hard time for me and I did not deal with that very well. I also did not know what to do or which direction to take.

But I knew poker was now becoming even more popular.

My good friend David Felton got in touch and explained

his car rental and van hire business had closed down and he was looking to get involved in a new venture.

I told him what I was doing with my shops and we decided to get one or two more shops together and make a go of it.

Although we planned it, I had no heart in it.

I realised that poker was the key part of my life and that I wasn't interested in anything except playing poker.

But I still needed an income ...

Me and David came up with an idea that we would supply poker products: tables, chips and other poker equipment. But we needed a well-known poker player who could be the face behind it.

We approached well-known TV player/former European champion Dave Colclough with a view to using his name to brand the products. We set up a meeting with him, but my partner was not sure he was the right person.

"Why don't we just market you?" he asked.

I felt I wasn't well known enough at the time because I needed more TV exposure.

But it was decided: Jonny Texas would become the name and brand - and I would be the face behind the products.

I managed to secure a place in a televised poker tournament run by Mad Marti Wilson. (Marti is currently working with Barry Hearne of Match Room Sports).

The tournament was being filmed at Maidstone Studios in Kent.

When the time came for me, Di and Dave Felton to travel to the studios, I found it hard to believe that here I was - going back in the studio to play cards again.

But this time I knew exactly what I was doing.

I was taken to a make-up room, had my makeup applied, had a microphone fixed to my shirt - and was then led to a table in the studio to play the greatest game in the world in front of a TV audience.

It felt unbelievable.

I knew I had to win. There was no way I was going to lose.

I was faced by Paul Jackson, the well-known Internet player called Action Jack. He had been a friend of mine playing at Walsall Casino in the West Midlands for many years. But he was now a household name and had become a good player.

Also on the programme was Ian Woodley - the first man to win a million on TV in Chris Evans's TFI Friday show.

Who Wants to be a Millionaire was out at the time, but Chris Evans was the first to give a million away.

I was also faced on the table with TV commentator/world class player from Ireland Pardrick Parson.

The cards were in the air. The dealer was told to 'shuffle and deal'. This was a well known phrase now, because the game was really big.

Within 30 minutes of play I had lost most of my stack of chips and was thinking 'how am I going to explain this'?

I needed Lady Luck to shine on me and for my patience to hold out.

All I was hoping was that I would not be the first to go out.

To my great surprise Paul Jackson was the first to leave - which made me feel more confident, invincible in fact.

It was time to push and become the aggressive player that I am known to be. So for the next four hours I pushed and bullied my way to a heads up situation with the great Pardrick.

The good thing was, I realised, I had made the end of the show no matter what. But I knew it would be hard now to beat Pardrick.

We shook hands and looked each other in the eyes and did a deal to save ten per cent of the winnings for the loser.

The dealer dealt and shuffled.

I was trying to go through my mind how I could beat Pardrick. I had the chip lead and thought: 'one hand and I could take him out'. But I was not sure how I would play this hand.

Before the last card was dealt I heard Pardrick say: "I'm all in."

As quick as I looked at my cards - before I had even looked at the second card I shouted: "Call."

My King and nine of spades was against his Jack and seven of clubs.

My God - the look on my face when the King came. It was all over and I had won. I felt very emotional.

It had suddenly dawned on me that my family and friends were all watching from the Green Room.

This day in 2005 was the start of my TV career in poker.

Chapter 24
China and a Whirl of TV

Me and Dave decided there was so much going on with poker and its products that we would go to the World Trade Fair in China.

I had never been there before, but Dave's girlfriend was Chinese and her mother ran an export business from China. This proved to be invaluable to us.

Dave flew out to Canton. Me and Di followed two days later, flying out from Gatwick.

After a 16-hour flight we arrived in Hong Kong - which was the biggest shock in my life. My reaction went something like: "Wow. Fucking hell."

It was just the phenomenal amount of people, life, cars, bustle - little people running all around me. I felt like a giant walking through those streets.

Slightly jet-lagged we checked into a basic hotel that Dave had booked us into.

Me and Dave left the girls at the hotel, then set off to see the sights. The plan was to leave Hong Kong the next day and get a visa to go to China.

It was a short train ride to where the visas were issued - where we spent six hours waiting for them to be approved. We were eventually granted 14-day visas, so we boarded a train, which took us to the border of China where it took us another two hours before we were allowed to cross.

We found border control very strict - no messing. They didn't let you in if they didn't like the look of you. Perhaps our border controls should be more like theirs.

Then we had another train ride, which took four and a half hours. During this train ride we noticed a massive change.

Suddenly Hong Kong seemed like heaven compared to where we went.

We arrived at a decent, comfortable hotel. The problem started when we decided to go and eat. We asked Dave's girlfriend Hayley to take us to a 'Chinese' restaurant.

I can only describe the food as live bugs - bowls of live bugs.

"Just give me chicken," I said. I lifted a chicken's head out of my curry........

There was a crab still walking on my table. It certainly wasn't like Mr Yong's Chinese down the road. A far cry from my local Chinese.

Suffice to say I lived on Pringles and Maltesers. I just could not eat the food. I found it terrible.

And I was shocked by the amount of poverty. There were small children begging in the streets. I gave them so much money. But I was told not to give them money because people would even break children's legs to get it off them.

I was about to give money to a tiny little old man who looked to me as if he was dying. But I was accosted by the police who told me not to. It was horrendous.

I feel China is moving forward at such a fast pace they need to stop and address the poor. There were high tower blocks everywhere, cars and fumes.

In one town Shinn Zen there were 70 million people - the whole population of Great Britain in one town.

When we eventually got to the fair we spent two days there.

The venue made Birmingham's National Exhibition Centre look tiny. It would take six weeks to walk round it. There was every product you could think of - from a thimble to an articulated lorry. And the Chinese would make anything for pennies.

The World Cup was coming up, so we ordered England flags with Jonny Texas logos on.

A deal was secured with a company to make poker tables for us. A meeting was then set up with Hayley's mother who would arrange for them to be shipped to England. The meeting was scheduled for Friday, but we brought it forward a day early because by this time I was desperate to get back to Hong Kong so I could eat something. I remember, back in Hong Kong, having the most beautiful steak and lobster meal overlooking the bay.

While I was in China I started negotiating with a Chinese government official about broadcasting poker TV shows in their country.

By this time we had a poker site almost set up on the net, so we were able to show him images of how it would look. This created great interest among the Chinese people.

We arrived back in England where we worked on getting all the logo designs ready for the tables. And we just concentrated on getting as many as we could into the UK.

The first order was for about £90-£100,000 worth of

stock. Me and Dave just decided to get the stock shipped in. We hadn't worried about selling it.

By now the poker site was up and running properly. And in the first two weeks all the signs were that it would make good money.

We were also approached for becoming sponsors of the world Heads-Up poker championship in Barcelona in 2006, and we thought this would give the site maximum publicity. The tournament was to be televised in over 70 countries - and the Jonny Texas name would be on the centre of the tables. It cost us about a quarter of a million, but what a waste of money. The tournament didn't get the airtime we expected and we only picked up about 200 new members on the website.

Over the next two to three months we were constantly checking prototypes sent over from China and were busy taking orders for tables and chips from local pubs holding tournaments.

In the meantime I was still travelling all over Europe playing poker, so Dave and Hayley did the day-to-day running of the company.

I travelled to Ireland for one particular match and while I was there I met the actor Patrick Murray who plays Mickey Pearce in Only Fools and Horses. I was just so excited to meet such a big name on such a popular TV show. I asked him if he would be prepared to wear a Jonny Texas T shirt and a deal was done. I flew him back to England and he attended a poker tournament.

I told Dave I had brought him something very special back from Ireland. He thought I meant a medal.

It turned into a very successful night. So Mickey had joined the Jonny Texas team.

The next celebrity to join us was Michael Grecco who played Pepi in Eastenders.

The idea was to bring celebrities in to every tournament. This would attract interest, people would take pictures - and the celeb's would be wearing Jonny Texas T shirts for the photos.

By this time invitations to TV shows were coming in thick and fast.

On one TV show filmed in London I reacted in absolute disbelief when I found out I was playing against one of my heroes - Teddy Sherringham!

I actually said to him: "I just can't believe I'm playing with you!"

Poker had now got me right into the dragon's den, playing with someone who was a hero to me, someone who had been a massive part of my life. To sit there playing poker with him was phenomenal.

So there I was playing my hero and he had set out to beat me. He flipped a set of eights, (three of a kind) a big hand. I bluffed them off him.

He had actually said on TV: "You wouldn't do that to me would you?"

Of course I would. The problem was he'd invited me to watch him play against West Ham. I had visions of 20,000 West Ham fans wanting to kill me!

Teddy bumped into me at another event later on and remembered how I bluffed him.

"That is exactly what poker is about," he said.

Which is why I am a pro' player and he is not.

The late Mike Read was great at poker, so was the rugby player Austin Healey. Most soccer players are good at playing poker - so is world champion darts player Phil Taylor. The list goes on: endless celebrities, even Big Brother contestants.

I was invited to play a game in a Barry Hearne production in the States. I had built a good relationship with multi millionaire boxing/snooker promoter Barry and he invited me to play in the Palms Casino, Vegas in December '06.

The idea of the tournament was the USA v Rest of the World. It was filmed by USA and UK channels. The teams included some of the best players in Europe.

After the tournament I was sitting waiting for the plane with Barry when he handed me an envelope.

"Carry this for me Jonny," he said. He handed me a parcel of at least £100,000! That was his win from the night before. Just his little joke, winding me up.....

Barry is such a clever businessman and one of the nicest guys you could meet.

I was also being helped by 'mad Marti Wilson' - who is now well established as tournament director with Barry Hearne. Marti was now becoming very well known in the poker world and was helping me in a big way by putting my poker tables into various tournaments around England, plus on a huge cruise liner on which he held tournaments.

So the brand name Jonny Texas was growing bigger and bigger - providing an income while I played poker with all its ups and downs.

It was a whirlwind during this period, and still is.

Chapter 25
A personal message to you

I would like to pause here for a moment and talk from the heart to you. Some of what I have to say may sound odd from a habitual gambler, but this is honestly what I feel.

I feel gambling is now being made far too easy in our society.

But the problem is not being given the attention it deserves.

Resources are put into solving other problems, such as domestic violence. But husbands can beat wives because of a gambling addiction. It's the same sort of disease - yes disease.

People gamble in all sorts of ways: with their lives sometimes by taking drugs, having affairs or driving fast cars. But there are a lot of couples out there, some with children, where gambling is a real problem.

Now children are taking to gambling. They can even have their own Solo credit cards and use them to gamble on the Internet - without anyone policing this.

And the situation is going to get worse.

Gambling in all its various forms is now commonplace with bookmakers, the lottery, the Internet and Solo machines - with people spending more than they can afford. Now there is talk of a 'super casino'.

I run a poker site, but I govern it. If I see someone going in too big and losing too much money I pull them off the site. I don't want people to lose their homes through gambling - I know from personal experience about that.

We can all get credit cards and spend 'easy money'. Where is it going to end? And what will it do to society? We need to wake up.

The whole gambling situation has got to be better policed and there needs to be more help groups, set up by people who understand. I would even be prepared to help set up these groups in my own area and speak to individuals myself. If just a quarter of the energy put into setting up gambling opportunities were put into help groups this would be something.

Big corporate organisations are giving us the gambling drug. It is even being advertised on TV and at football matches around the pitch and on players' shirts - which could have a huge influence on youngsters.

Efforts have been made to ban smoking, but gambling can be far worse, leading to debt, divorce and violence.

Call me a hypocrite because I run my own gambling Internet site, but I want people to enjoy the game. You don't have to bet with real money. You can play with chips - or even trade off, whoever loses having to mow the lawn - like me and Di do when we play card games.

Gambling sites should have links to Gamblers' Anonymous. And more of the cash made should be ploughed back into local causes.

I have been very, very lucky. People see the glitz and the TV appearances. But for every ten gamblers there are nine very miserable people and fat cats getting richer.

You are not going to stop a habitual gambler, but you can show that person how to manage the addiction. So a support group would have to be set up with a new approach. I believe gamblers even get a buzz, an adrenalin rush, from losing.

A gambler always sets himself or herself a challenge. But over a period of time the fact is - they will lose.

Chapter 26
Programme makers and back to Vegas

Another adventure.

Me and Dave decided we should make our own poker TV shows. So we approached a TV company, which was struggling for cash but had a platform on a Sky TV network, and we managed to agree a deal - broadcasting shows from their studios on an Asian channel.

It was run by strict Muslims who frown on gambling - so we paid an excessive amount of money to Raj TV studio in Birmingham.

A deal was done to use their facility any time and make our TV shows. Craig was employed as tournament director. We built the set and employed a cameraman - then got together 72 of the best poker players in the country.

We called the event The Jonny Texas Invitation Open. To me it was a way of making money and getting the Jonny Texas name out there.

We had the poker tables made and Craig ran the tournament for us. We supplied the best food for all the players and held a knockout tournament - where I made it to the final.

I was a bit perturbed by all the big names there and wanted it to go well. My friend Barry Hearne was there, as well as one of the best online players in the world, Paul Jackson.

My good friend Anthony Nicholls was on board, and it was just great to see people supporting me and running it.

It cost over £70,000 and took about four months to plan the tournament. There was total prize money of £100,000 - all of which we put up. We financed the whole show and prize money for the players.

The tournament was won by Paul Jackson.

When we came to edit the show the sound quality was all mixed up so the programme did not go on air. In the end we lost over £60,000 and me and Dave felt about £90,000 had been wasted.

But we did it, we pulled it off and the tournament itself was a success. If we had got good quality sound we would have had airtime, so we just put it down to experience.

That's TV world. It gets a bit weary sometimes.

Anyway, in 2006 life was one round of tournaments and in July it was back to Vegas for the World Championships.

There was me, Di, Mickey Pearce, Dave and Craig Wildman.

Craig has been a friend of mine for nearly 20 years back to the days of the clutch centre. I used to see him then in a Walsall town centre casino, which was owned by a mutual friend Phil Sanders.

Craig was good company and a great laugh. He is a very experienced poker player and has a great disciplined mind when it comes to playing the game.

But there was even more exciting and challenging stuff this year. Craig, Dave and Pat followed us a week later.

Because of my success on TV people were really backing me to do well in this event. And there was a million pound prize money for the winner.

When I arrived in Vegas I could not believe all the hype. Not only was it still there, it was getting bigger and bigger and bigger.

Some tournaments even had 3,000 people sitting down to play. There were about 50-60,000 people there, taking part in many different tournaments.

It was obvious to me: Vegas is now the Mecca of poker, THE place to be. I checked into the MGM Grand Hotel and before I even unpacked my case I was downstairs taking part in my first game.

For the first time ever I had to wait to get onto a cash table. That's how much poker had really grown. It also seemed to be full of young USA college kids who all thought they had the amazing ability of mind reading other players. Before long I was sat at a table enjoying the banter, the goading - and the bullshit from these college kids who are a breed of their own.

This was a new breed of player. And the fact that not many people knew me in the States (or so I thought) gave me a great opportunity to exercise some of my aggressive moves on them. Within six hours of play I had amassed my first $4-5,000. But this can actually be bad. I prefer to start bad and go up.

But I did enjoy the game.

Little did I know some of my games had been shown in

the States, so I did actually get recognised. My cover was blown! So I went upstairs to unpack.

Playing poker is not like playing golf against the world number one. In poker there's an element of skill and a lot of luck. When your luck deserts you and you put your money in with your best hand, and lady luck does not shine on you, you could be playing with a guy who has only played for a week and he could win.

Sometimes I wish I could go back to playing when no-one knew me - I could win more easily in those days. Now I have the biggest target on my back. They want to knock Jonny Texas out. It's as if I have a bounty on my head. Now I'm even known abroad: the price of fame.

Many a time I've wanted to play with a false beard and big hat! I've even tried travelling to casinos away from home.

Sometimes when people do beat me they say: "I saw you play that on the telly!"

When a poker show is made, the game could have lasted seven hours with 115 hands dealt. But on TV it's shown for an hour with 12 or 15 hands. Editors obviously like to show hands that people would not normally play. They want to show hands where the tournament is on the line or where only lady luck can win the game.

You could have a guy who can only win on a ten of diamonds say - and it comes. These are what they show on TV.

There's a saying 'a blind pig will always find its way to the trough'. They will win and always beat you in these tournaments.

When I started playing poker I was just happy-go-lucky. I had no idea it was going to get this big. People actually get paid if they beat me at charity dos.

But I often now play tournaments where I have a game I can't lose and deliberately give off so many signals. One guy actually got up and shook my hand and told me: "The pleasure of saying I played with you is more fun than winning the tournament!"

Poker has surprised me where everything else failed, though I don't think I was really bad. It's a far cry from mum and dad sending me for help and attending gamblers' anonymous.

How the tables have turned. Once it was frowned upon and you would not tell people you played poker. There was no such thing as a professional poker player years ago. It was just money in your pocket with your mates.

Now it's the glitzy lifestyle.

Chapter 27
For Great Britain

By this time I had created an impressive record, having won seven out of eight televised tournaments.

One morning at 10am the phone rang. It was Dave Devilfish Ulliott who I had known for about 15 years. He is of the greatest poker players not just in Britain but in the world. Dave is particularly known as a formidable poker player in the USA and Europe.

"What are you doing next week?" he asked.

Then he went on to say that what he had to tell me must be a secret. He said that due to my success on TV he had decided to pick me to represent Great Britain playing poker on a TV show for Channel 4 that was to be filmed in Wales.

But what did sadden me was my mentor, European champion Mickey had not been selected. It felt awkward that I had been picked and he had not.

I have since found out that he and Dave had some sort of misunderstanding over a magazine article. Dave felt that Mickey had slandered him. Anyway, it left a bit of a bad taste. I just hoped I had been chosen on my own merit. I even pulled Dave aside on the day of filming to ask him why I had been chosen. He repeated it was because of my successful performances.

This was a big stage for me - against the best poker players in the world. It was a six-handed TV format game.

Team USA was captained by Robert Williamson III. The team included Phil Laack (known as The Uni Bomber), Antonio Estefan (The Magician) and Jennifer Tilly (Hollywood actress and world women's bracelet winner).

The Dutch team was captained by Marcel Luske.

There were teams from Sweden, Norway and Germany: six players from each country playing against each other for the Six Nations Cup. And I had possibly the hardest draw - against Phil, the Uni Bomber. Phil, possibly the most fascinating player, sat next to me. A mathematical genius, he was a perfect gentleman.

It was possibly the most important game in my life - a very, very nerve-racking match. I was representing Great Britain and I knew I had to do well. There was also a personal pride at stake as well.

The winning team would take £100,000 to be shared. Each player that won a heat would take £12,000.

I had a very nervous start. I managed to pick up one or two decent hands. Within one hour I had got into a situation with a pair of aces - against the Uni bomber who had ace king. And I knocked him out. I knew then if I could beat him I could go on and win the game.

I finally got heads up with a guy from Sweden. The game against him lasted two and a half hours - but I eventually became the winner of my heat.

After the game I walked into the green room where my family and friends were cheering - only to be pulled aside by Devilfish who spent ten minutes going through a long list of things I had done wrong!

That is exactly what I would have expected of him though. And he did congratulate me ...

After winning my heat the UK went into the finals of chip leaders. Dave wanted to pick me for the final match, but was outvoted. Four of the six England players won their heats and Great Britain finished third.

The next opportunity to play for Great Britain will be in 2008, but Devilfish did not get picked as captain. Subsequently, Roland de Wolfe who had shown great form over the last 12 months (who I do find to be a very nice person), chose his own friends to play for the Great Britain team, which is typical of poker players' attitudes.

This was another major step, another chapter of my life.

When you are playing poker, when you are in the zone: the environment, the atmospheric buzz, the adrenalin rush all carries you in a false emotion. If I lose a tournament I have to get out of the atmosphere. I will even walk back to the hotel.

But to have been selected to play for the Great Britain team with the best line-up in the world, to prove myself on national TV, was unbelievable to me.

I realised a lot of people would be watching and, looking at the line-up of players and the distances some of them had travelled, I felt 'should I be here?'

It felt strange to have 30 or 40 people running round me preparing for the show to go on air.

I had gone from travelling to the Rainbow for a £10 competition on a Friday night over 20 years ago to playing for my country. It was one hell of a massive step. Imagine if someone had predicted all this years ago when I was sneaking off to play so my wife wouldn't know ...

The highlight came when we were all asked to sign our shirts and money was going to be raised for charity from the sale of the shirts.

I had already started to do charity work, so it was a good thing to get this TV exposure. People were starting to recognise me - only those interested in poker obviously.

You would be surprised how much TV impacts on people. By being on TV people seem to think you are some sort of massive celebrity.

When I walk in the newly opened Casino now it's by invitation and people whisper and stare because they know who I am.

To think I used to sneak into the place when it was the old dark, dingy Casino. You would never imagine the current situation would be feasibly possible.

It doesn't do your game any good though because everyone wants to beat you. They take more chances because they are so desperate to beat you.

I often ask myself why people watch poker on TV. What can be the interest? The funny thing is, it's not only in Great Britain, this interest is happening across Europe and all over the world.

Having six nations descend on Cardiff in Wales tells me there is something in this great game.

I have been playing poker for over 20 years. Times have changed - and I have changed with the times.

Around this time I put my name forward for the charity Weston Spirit run by Falklands veteran Simon Weston and

I raised £700 by hosting a poker evening - which was nice because it wasn't all about gambling. People could have fun and a charity would benefit.

Because of my image on TV, I would be flown to Belfast or Blackpool for charity events - and people would come.

Poker is just growing and growing, being played in pubs because TV had made it so popular. And by now it was going at such a pace that I would be getting paid just to make an appearance. Who knows where it will take me next?

After all the lows I had become heartily sick of things going wrong. But surely you can only fail so many times. I am a firm believer that you have to fail to succeed - so it seemed as if I had been waiting all this time for something to go right.

Chapter 28
Pub Poker Takes a Tumble

Due to the success of my business selling poker tables manufactured in China I began being approached by several people interested in setting up their own pub poker challenges.

They bought our Jonny Texas tables and set up poker nights across the Midlands, and it really became a success. I attended one of two of the events where people reacted with disbelief because I had attended in person. It seems I gave a real boost to their night if they knew I was going to turn up and the organisers would get more people in.

I find it quite flattering that these people would turn up to see me.

Some of the pubs were starting to get 30-40 people regularly, which was great for us. It meant more people were seeing the logo and logging onto the website. The pubs were busy selling more beer - and everyone was doing well out of the arrangement. I was happy because it reminded me of the old days of poker. It was fun again for me to play.

It fascinates me the way poker has grown. You can sit round a table with people in their 80s, no matter what creed, colour, disability, background, nationality - all on a level playing field. It's the only sport in the world where you haven't got to be super fit. You don't even have to have a talent. You can learn it. It's not like being a snooker player with a natural ability. I think that's what the attraction is.

Technically it was illegal to play in pubs, but landlords were turning a blind eye as long as they were selling beer. So these pub poker nights started springing up all over the country. They were only on a small scale with an entrance fee of about £2.50 and top prize money of about £100, though some are still holding tournaments with higher stakes.

Everything was going well - until I had a phone call asking me to see the manager of my local casino in Walsall.

I went to the casino and the manager sat me down and said: "It's been brought to our attention that you may be helping poker tournaments across the county in pubs. This is in direct competition."

Actually I wasn't running poker nights, I was just selling products that the pubs were using.

I was horrified that I might be banned from the casino where all my ranking tournaments are held. I told the manager I was shocked that he got the impression I was running the poker nights and explained they were just using my products.

I was aware that people would go around and check these nights, so I even had to shy away even from presenting trophies at pub poker nights. This could have created major problems for me otherwise.

Now, since the smoking ban and efforts to reduce poker in pubs I hear 200 pubs a month across the country are going into bankruptcy.

I would have liked to have been involved in setting new clubs up, but had to stick to selling tables and chips. I couldn't really understand it - especially as one casino manager approached me and said a load of new members had joined because they had been to one of these Jonny Texas pub evenings, so it had done some good for that casino.

Pub poker nights are a good way to learn, but I do have some worries about the illegal type of games though - that they aren't being policed correctly. I worry about people creaming off the profits.

There is money to be made out of poker nights. The famous TV programme Dragon's Den showed that.

There was a guy who went on with the idea of opening a poker pub league. He had all three dragons desperate to invest in it ...

Chapter 29
Europe

I have now travelled to most European countries as each one hosts a major tournament.

In 2007 it was the turn of Poland. I had wanted to visit Poland, so the tournament was a great opportunity to kill two birds with one stone.

I flew from Birmingham Airport to Warsaw with my good friend Richard Chamberlain. Richard has been a close friend in my life. He has been with me to Poland and the USA and has been a really good friend, someone I have always been able to talk to. Richard is very much like me - always lived a life of gambling. Our lives were spent playing in local snooker halls, living day by day.

I found Poland to be an amazing place. The people were so friendly. The hotel cost me the equivalent of about £79 a night - but it was like a £700 a night hotel because of the difference in cost of living there. I can see why Polish people come to England. Although everything is so cheap in their country the wages are not very high.

I arrived at the hotel really excited and went to see where the tournament was being held. It turned out to be in another great hotel round the corner. It cost about £5,000 to play. So I paid the entrance and had an early night.

At the tournament there was much hype and high fives, and people were glad to see me.

I lasted four minutes! I was out within the first two hands.

You can travel all the way there, it can cost about £6,000 with expenses - and it can really deflate you.

You can travel five or six hours on a plane and sit down to play for one minute. So you learn to plan your trip in case you are knocked out pretty quickly.

I had planned to visit the German prisoner of war camps - not that I have a morbid fascination.

I got a taxi driver who must have thought it was his lucky day. I asked him to drive us to Auschwitz which cost us about £200 there and back. The driver spoke perfect English and he took us to all these restaurants, so it became more of a sightseeing trip.

To all those people who have not been to Auschwitz:

My God.

I was told there were no birds there, no life. It was scary. Worse than quiet - lifeless.

The liberation of the Jews and all that involves is a big part of our history, but more so to my father's generation.

To my children it probably doesn't mean much. Children nowadays have no association with that war. To them, war is what is going on in Iraq or Iran.

But to my grandfathers who fought in the war it is different.

There were thousands of visitors at Auschwitz. There was so much crying. People in their 80s were walking around there, people who had been prisoners. It was unbelievable.

Despite this I'm glad I went.

Before I went there I thought of it as just a place to visit. Now I realise I should have taken it a lot more seriously.

It was definitely not a day trip to Alton Towers. You would not want to go with a packed lunch and a camera.

Also in 2007 I attended a tournament in my favourite city in the world, Barcelona. In fact one of my fondest memories is of Man U winning the European Cup there.

I debated whether to go at all because my grandmother (my mum's mum) had been quite ill and was in hospital. I was very close to her, so decided to visit her at Good Hope Hospital, Sutton Coldfield, then go to the tournament, flying out on my own and coming straight back.

When I arrived in Barcelona the next day I checked into a small hotel and had some time to stroll the streets and take in the atmosphere. The city means a lot to me. I love the culture, the buildings, and I understand some Spanish from my time in Majorca. I visited the Ramblers, a tourist site and sat there enjoying a coffee and thinking about happy times in Barcelona - and about the tournament which was due to start at 2pm.

When I arrived at the tournament I looked at the draw and knew one of two of the faces. There was the usual banter and chat, and the atmosphere was very exciting. I had paid £5,000 to enter.

One person out of about 400 entrants was going to walk away nearly a millionaire, with three quarters of a million.

When you have won tournaments like that you know you can be one of those winners. But 400 people are thinking the same …

It was a very unusual day. All day I felt something was not right, but I didn't know what it was.

I phoned my mum and said: "How is gran?"

I could tell in her voice something was not right.

"You've got to remember your gran is old now," she said. "She has had a good life."

The tournament started and I won my first hand.

The next hand a guy made a bet. I bet. The hand played out …

On the last move I said: "I'm all in" (which means the tournament is on the line).

I was playing a Scandinavian - who thought about his next move for a full eight minutes deciding whether to call me. It felt like a lifetime - especially as I was bluffing. There was no way he could have known, but he called me.

I was just so pissed off I had made this bet that I got up and walked away from the table, switched my phone off, went to the hotel, got my clothes, got on a plane and flew straight into Birmingham. Within three hours I was home.

When I got back to Birmingham I switched my phone back on and there were about ten messages from poker players:

"Where are you? You have still got chips. You're still in the tournament!"

I just could not believe it.

But it was just like an act of God, something very strange.

My gran died that night and I was able to be with her.

When you are young you take people for granted. Gran lived in Shard End, Birmingham, and was a big part of my life when I was growing up.

I realised I had been very lucky to be in my forties and still have a gran. She was 87. Most of my friends have not got their mothers, least of all a gran. I was very privileged.

Chapter 30
What a Life

My life has not been a normal one.

People don't understand what a gambler is, like I don't understand what it's like to be a drug addict or an alcoholic.

But I can empathise with them.

An addict or an alcoholic would spend their last pound on drink or drugs. That's exactly what a gambler would do - spend that last pound on a bet. They get just as much buzz out of losing as winning. If you win it's a bonus.

A gambler spends most of his or her life getting an adrenaline rush from an endorphin called Nor. Eventually, when you get to your 40s or 50s this does you harm and can affect the nervous system. I've seen it in a lot of people as they get older. They are on edge, nervous.

I said earlier in the book that I wanted to talk more about my brother Colin, a gambler. But he is now so ill that it doesn't seem right to say any more.

How have I escaped? Some people are blessed.

I have tried never to deprive my family. Gambling has not been the be all and end all. I have not had to put my last £1 on to win. I would give my last £1 away rather than gamble it. I can't walk past people who beg - particularly if they are outside a casino!

The other night after a tournament in Nottingham I intended to stop for fish and chips, but there was this guy begging.

He said: "I honestly don't drink. The Big Issue has not been printed because of Christmas."

He was looking for a couple of quid for food. I gave him my last five quid and went home and made a sandwich.

I remember my dad telling people how when I was 14 I took the telly from our front room and leant it to a man down the road because he didn't have a TV.

So then we didn't have one!

Things have really moved on.

My precious little daughter Alexis has decided to leave the nest. I'm very proud of her. She's met a lovely guy called Richard and they have bought a little flat a mile down the road in Cannock.

Alexis is a great nursery nurse. She is always getting gifts and presents off the kids. Alexis is a very lovable child and I love her dearly.

Jonathan is 21 and still at Leicester University. He is like his dad!

He's done a nine-week reality show for Channel 4 called Shipwrecked. The show, which had him left on an island, was aired in March 2008. Jonathan was lucky enough to win over £5,000 as his team, 'The Tigers' won! He is already talking about getting an agent and going into TV.

My eldest son Matt is 22 and lives with his girlfriend Joanne and their daughter Ruby in a flat nearby. Matt originally wanted a career in gambling, but now just goes to the bookies. He enjoys playing poker at home with me and our friends. Matt thinks he is a great poker player!

I wouldn't want any of my children to be gamblers. The only one I thought would be was Matt. But I'm glad to say he hasn't gone down that road. He has gone into labouring. He is like my brother Colin, a grafter, and will work with his hands, Matt and his girlfriend are expecting tehri second child at the time of writing.

In January 2008, me and Di celebrated having been together for 25 years. She is still my rock, putting up with my temper and mood swings.

And what of the future?

I still want to discourage people from gambling. It's been made too easy and I would like to see more done about that - otherwise we are going to have a serious meltdown.

The only people getting rich are bookies who have become big corporations. Imagine if a drug dealer said they were going to open up super drug dens. (Though I believe the biggest cause of problems in this country is drink, the cause of fights and deaths on the road).

Now you can get credit cards and gamble online. Any kid on a laptop can do it and it's not policed at all.

I am actually thinking about packing it all in and getting a job. I can see myself selling the name Jonny Texas. I would like to be a social worker or a policeman (it takes a crook to catch a crook).

In the meantime there are loads of tournaments. I'm still doing a lot, and I've done a lot. There's going to be nothing left to do when I'm an old man. Then I can sit back and take a rest.

I'm now 46 and when you get older you sit back and look

at things differently. I have been gambling for over 40 years so don't know much else.

I want to get more charity events going and hope to play for Great Britain again. I would like to win a world ranking event.

Di no longer travels with me and I can't see that changing in the future because of the grandchildren. So I do go on my own a lot now.

But there are so many Prima Donnas in poker - so many arseholes, and kids saying 'I won so and so'.

I am in the top 50 all time players in Great Britain, the 72nd biggest money earner in Great Britain for playing poker.

There are even re-runs of games which I have been involved in being shown on TV.

I only need to win one major tournament now. With a major win I could end up in the top five.

But I could pack it all up tomorrow. It's expensive, with some tournaments costing £200,000 a year just to enter.

I have got to that stage now where if I peak at things I like to bow out. I need to win half a million - then I would pack up.

There have been recent good times.

Me and Micky Wernick had been apart for a while and tended to only see each other at tournaments. But I recently picked him up and we went to Nottingham together. It was so great travelling there together and chatting like in the old days.

While we were at the tournament the management actually stopped the competition and pointed us out. Dave

Blondi Colclough was also with us.

The management said: "On table C1 we have possibly three of the best world class poker players. Between them they have won three and a half million!"

Everyone gave us a round of applause.

I was having a bit of a rough spell and Mickey was doing his usual: "Are you playing your 'A' game?"

I came fifth in that tournament, which I was quite pleased with.

My dream would be to set up a charity for gamblers, so that when they are really under we bail them out - pay the mortgage etc. But would that encourage them to gamble more?

If we did that, it would have to be their last hope. And they would have to agree to attend a programme to rebuild their lives.

There are some desperate situations, and nothing exists at the moment like that. If there is someone out there who is interested in starting up a scheme like that - contact me.

I would also like to invent 'The One Percent Club' and get it known nationally. People who were part of the club could wear a little gold badge.

The idea is for them to donate one per cent of their wins to charity. I would like every poker player in the country to be registered in the club. There are millions a year given away in prize money. If you win say £10,000, £100 would be donated to charity.

In particular I would like to support a cancer charity and the homeless. But it would have to be run right.

I would also like to set up a charity for the mothers, wives and children of gamblers, the innocent people in this. There are people out there who have lost everything through no fault of their own.

In ten years' time I'd like to be living in Las Vegas, playing poker somewhere where I can hide more easily. I like playing poker where people don't know me. But gamblers don't plan. They don't know.

In Birmingham recently there was this hoodie type kid who spotted me and he kept saying 'Are you Jonny Texas? Are you Jonny Texas?"

"Sometimes," I told him.

I actually asked him if he was taking the piss at one point, but he swore he wasn't. Even on the motorway people hang out of car windows, shouting and waving when they recognise me.

I would like to go back to when I could play cards and get money - instead of everyone wanting to gamble with me. People bet with me because they want to beat me - just so they can say they have beaten Jonny Texas.

Some years ago a guy who had played against me and lost, rang me and admitted he knew there was no way he could win.

"Why did you play then?" I asked him.

"Because at least I could say I lost to you!" he said.

I would really like to be anonymous - but I know that's not going to happen.

I have not been an angel all my life, but I do have things to be proud of.

I am proud of my three children.

I am most proud of my Great Britain win, the highlight.

I am most proud to have met some great people and proud to have been part of the growth of poker.

But you can't ask a gambler what he'll be doing in ten years' time.

Ask me what I'll be doing tomorrow.

Chapter 31
Life Now ...

During 2008 I did some work for various charities, including fundraisers for SCOPE which raises awareness and money for sufferers of cerebral palsy.

My daugher Alexis had her baby in May '08 - and how ironic - little Lacey may be suffering from cerebral palsy.

Alexis spent three-four days in slow labour. When Lacey was eventually born I had been sitting outside the labour room at Staffordshire General Hospital for nearly 14 hours. At 11.50pm I had a text from Di to say that Alexis had given birth (Di and Richard, Alexis's boyfriend, had been with her throughout). But within four to five minutes of Lacey being born I heard alarms going off and even though there were other girls in there I just knew there were problems with Alexis's baby.

Di came out crying and told me there were complications. There seemed to be a lot of panic on the faces of doctors and nurses. I had been standing outside that room holding two balloons, one pink one blue, like a fucking idiot.

Over the next two-three days Lacey suffered severe seizures - yet we spent 24 hours waiting trying to get her a bed in a specialist unit. It horrifies me that in Great Britain in 2008 we don't have enough beds for children born with complications. At one time the nearest bed was in Scotland. It was even more stressful because we realised that the only way a bed would become available would be through the misfortune of someone else's child not making it. This just added stress to the situation.

I am not a religious man but during this whole experience was the one time I literally prayed.

Me and Di were heartbroken in what was to have been a time of pure excitement. For me and Di to see Alexis's face, knowing her child had been born with complications, is possibly the worse time of our lives.

It was only the support of very good friends which got us through and I would like to thank them very much.

Lacey was eventually admitted to an intensive care unit for babies at St Mary's Hospital in Manchester and the work they do there is tremendous.

We are now playing a waiting game with Lacey's future.

So 2008: Lacey being born, my dad has been quite ill and the world is in recession.

I went to Vegas to play poker in '08, but only for nine days, because my heart was not in it. I almost didn't even board the plane because this was shortly after Lacey was born and that really rocked my whole world.

Since then my mind has not been on poker.

And with all the stress I have started smoking again.

Sadly, while writing this book I also learned of the death of a good friend who helped me during my time share days in Majorca - Robert Murray. Robert passed away on July 31 '08 from a heart attack aged 48.

It's funny, but whatever pattern of life you choose you

always associate with people of your own sort - and mine have always been gamblers.

The biggest mistake of my life is I only ever associated with gamblers, people who have mood swings: big ups and big lows - but more lows than ups.

And I still believe we are going to have a serious problem in the future with children gambling.

I am probably maturing: I realise there are no winners in gambling.

www.apexpublishing.co.uk